EinFach Englisch
Unterrichtsmodell

Series Editor: Hans Kröger

Slumdog Millionaire

by
Meike Strohn
Lisa Rauschelbach

edited by
Hans Kröger

Vorwort

 Einzelarbeit

 Partnerarbeit

 Gruppenarbeit

 Unterrichtsgespräch

 Schreibauftrag

 Hausaufgabe

 filmische Präsentation

 Projekt, offene Aufgabe

 kreative Aufgabe

 szenisches Spiel, Rollenspiel

Der Titel der Reihe **EinFach Englisch** verdeutlicht Zielsetzung und Programm zugleich. Einerseits soll Schülerinnen und Schülern auf einfache Art und Weise der Zugang zu klassischen, aber auch neuen literarischen Werken und Filmen ermöglicht werden, andererseits sollen Lehrerinnen und Lehrern in der Praxis erprobte Unterrichtsmodelle angeboten werden, die die wichtigsten methodisch-didaktischen Ansätze ihres Faches Englisch abdecken. Dabei sind die Modelle direkt, ohne langes Einlesen einsetzbar und stellen Unterrichtsarbeit konkret vor. Als besonders hilfreich für die Praxis haben sich dabei folgende Aspekte erwiesen, die für die Gestaltung der Reihe wesentlich sind:

- Überblick über **Figurenkonstellation**, ggf. **Filmszenen** und **Inhalt**
- **Klausuren** mit **Erwartungshorizont**
- **Arbeitsblätter**, **Tafelbilder** und **Leitfragen** für den Unterricht
- **Piktogramme** als Hinweise auf **Unterrichts-** und **Arbeitsformen**

Das Prinzip der „**Components**" ermöglicht darüber hinaus den variablen Einsatz der Modelle in unterschiedlich konzipierten Unterrichtsreihen. Dabei stehen Machbarkeit und Praxisnähe stets im Vordergrund.

Das vorliegende Modell bezieht sich auf die britische DVD-Version *Slumdog Millionaire*, **Pathé/Celador Films/Film 4, 2008.**

Sprachliche Betreuung: Elin Arbin

westermann GRUPPE

© 2019 Bildungshaus Schulbuchverlage
Westermann Schroedel Diesterweg Schöningh Winklers GmbH, Braunschweig
www.westermann.de

Das Werk und seine Teile sind urheberrechtlich geschützt.
Jede Nutzung in anderen als den gesetzlich zugelassenen Fällen bedarf der
vorherigen schriftlichen Einwilligung des Verlages.
Für Verweise (Links) auf Internet-Adressen gilt folgender Haftungshinweis:
Trotz sorgfältiger inhaltlicher Kontrolle wird die Haftung für die Inhalte der
externen Seiten ausgeschlossen. Für den Inhalt dieser externen Seiten sind
ausschließlich deren Betreiber verantwortlich. Sollten Sie daher auf kostenpflichtige,
illegale oder anstößige Inhalte treffen, so bedauern wir dies ausdrücklich und bitten
Sie, uns umgehend per E-Mail davon in Kenntnis zu setzen, damit beim Nachdruck
der Verweis gelöscht wird.

Druck A^4 / Jahr 2019
Alle Drucke der Serie A sind im Unterricht parallel verwendbar.

Umschlaggestaltung: Jennifer Kirchhof
Druck und Bindung: Westermann Druck GmbH, Braunschweig

ISBN 978-3-14-**041189**-9

Getting started

Slumdog Millionaire

1. Der Film 6
2. Die Personen 8
3. Biographical information 10
4. Scene index 11
5. Vorüberlegungen zum Einsatz des Films im Unterricht 14
6. Klausuren 17
7. Konzeption des Unterrichtsmodells 23
8. Components 24
9. Bibliographische Hinweise 89

Component 1: Introducing a Slumdog's life 24

1.1 Pre-viewing activity: Film poster 24
1.2 Long-term while-viewing tasks 25
- Copy 1: Transparency – Pictures of film characters 27
- Copy 2: Worksheet – Long-term while-viewing tasks: Characters 28
- Copy 3: Worksheet – Long-term while-viewing task: Timeline of Jamal's life 30
- Copy 4: Worksheet – Long-term while-viewing tasks: Music & sound – possible effects 31

1.3 Content: *Who Wants to Be a Millionaire?* – novel into film 37
- Copy 5: Text – Q & A by Vikas Swarup 39

1.4 Background: The term "Slumdog" – discussing its connotations 40
- Copy 6: Text – The term "Slumdog" 41

1.5 Film analysis: Cinematic devices – *slum chase* 42
- Copy 7: Text – The language of film: Selected terms for film analysis 43
- Copy 8: Worksheet – While-viewing tasks: Cinematic devices 45

Component 2: The three musketeers: "All for one, one for all"? 49

2.1 Content: Taking a closer look at the three musketeers 49
- Copy 9: Worksheet – Jamal, Salim and Latika – their relationships 50

2.2 Background: The conflict between Hindus and Muslims in India 51
- Copy 10: Texts – Book excerpt and newspaper article 53

2.3 Film analysis: The depiction of the Hindu attack on the Muslim slum 52
- Copy 11: Audio commentary by Danny Boyle 56

Component 3: From Taj Mahal to Mumbai: A journey to the past   57

3.1 Content: Listening comprehension   57
- Copy 12: Worksheet – Who says what and in what context?   60

3.2 Background: Conducting an Internet research on Agra and Mumbai   59

3.3 Film analysis: Subjective viewpoint   61

Component 4: A roller coaster ride from rags to raja   63

4.1 Content   63

4.2 Background: Globalisation   64

4.3 Film analysis: Chapter 19   66
- Copy 13: Worksheet – Chapter 19: Film analysis   68

Component 5: A triangle of money, love, and destiny   69

5.1 Content: The ride of money, love, and destiny for Jamal and Salim   69
- Copy 14: Worksheet – Triangles of money, love, and destiny   71

5.2 Background: The song *Jai Ho*   72

5.3 Film analysis: Chapters 24–27   73

Component 6: Post-viewing activities   75

6.1 Presentation of *long-term while-viewing tasks*   75

6.2 Quiz questions in *WWM* format   75
- Copy 15: Quiz cards   77
- Copy 16: Quiz questions on "Who Wants to Be an Expert on *Slumdog Millionaire* and India?"   78
- Copy 17: Correct answers for quiz questions on "Who Wants to Be an Expert on *Slumdog Millionaire* and India?"   81
- Copy 18: Answer cards   84

6.3 Trailer   76

6.4 Film reviews   85
- Copy 19: Text – Film review: 'Is that your final answer?'   86
- Copy 20: Worksheet – How to write a review   88

5

Der Film

Der Film *Slumdog Millionaire* von Regisseur Danny Boyle kam im März 2009 in die deutschen Kinos. Er erhielt zahlreiche Auszeichnungen, wie beispielsweise acht Oscars, vier Golden Globes und mehrere Publikumspreise. *Slumdog Millionaire* basiert auf dem 2005 erschienenen Roman *Q & A* von Vikas Swarup.

Der Film handelt von dem 18-jährigen Jamal, einem Jungen aus den Slums von Mumbai, der von der Polizei verhört und gefoltert wird, da er im Verdacht steht, bei der Teilnahme an der indischen Version der Quiz-Show *Wer wird Millionär?* betrogen zu haben. Tatsächlich hat er jedoch jede Quizfrage korrekt beantwortet, da sich die Fragen zufällig auf Ereignisse aus seinem Leben bezogen haben. Jamal hat allerdings nicht an der Show teilgenommen, um Millionär zu werden, sondern um die Liebe seines Lebens, Latika, wiederzufinden. Durch den Einsatz von Rückblenden erzählt der Film die Geschichte von Jamal, seinem Bruder Salim und Latika. Dabei wird diese Geschichte verflochten mit Szenen aus der Polizeiwache, in der Jamal verhört wird, und mit Szenen, die Jamal während seiner Teilnahme an *Wer wird Millionär?* zeigen.

Der chronologische Beginn der Geschichte erzählt von den siebenjährigen Brüdern Jamal und Salim, deren Mutter bei einem Angriff von Hindus auf ihr muslimisches Slum getötet wird. Die beiden Waisen lernen die gleichaltrige Latika kennen, mit der Jamal sich auf Anhieb gut versteht. Nachdem die drei Waisen sich eine Zeit lang auf einer Müllhalde durchgeschlagen haben, werden sie von dem skrupellosen Gangster Maman aufgelesen, der sie in sein Camp bringt. Dort leben Dutzende von Kindern, die zu professionellen Bettlern ausgebildet werden und für Maman arbeiten. Salim wird Zeuge eines schrecklichen Ereignisses: Einem Jungen namens Arvind wird von Mamans Mitarbeitern sogar das Augenlicht genommen, damit er beim Betteln mehr Geld verdient. Daraufhin flüchten Salim und Jamal, während Latika die Flucht aus dem Camp nicht gelingt, was nicht zuletzt Salims Schuld ist. Obwohl die beiden Brüder zunächst streiten, da Jamal Latika vermisst und zu ihr zurückkehren möchte, arbeiten die beiden dann doch zusammen, um Geld zu verdienen: Sie verkaufen verschiedene Dinge in einem Zug, mit dem sie schließlich nach Agra gelangen.

Die Jungen sind nun 13 Jahre alt, verdienen ihr Geld als angebliche Reiseführer im Taj Mahal und nebenbei als Taschendiebe. Da Jamal Latika noch immer vermisst, machen sich die Brüder auf den Weg zurück nach Mumbai, um dort nach ihr zu suchen. Sie finden sie im Rotlichtviertel, wo sie von Maman und seiner Gang als Tänzerin trainiert wird. Bei der gemeinsamen Flucht werden die drei von Maman überrascht, den Salim kaltblütig erschießt, damit die drei flüchten und nebenbei noch Mamans Geld mitnehmen können. Während Jamal und Latika über ihre Beziehung sprechen, heuert Salim bei Gangsterboss Javed an. Als Salim zu Jamal und Latika zurückkehrt, wirft er seinen Bruder hinaus, um Latika für sich zu haben.

Nach einem weiteren mehrjährigen Zeitsprung zeigt der Film Jamal als nun 18-jährigen jungen Mann, der als Servicekraft in einer englischsprachigen Telekommunikationsfirma arbeitet. Von dort sucht er nach Latika und ruft seinen Bruder an. Die beiden treffen sich und reden über die Vergangenheit. Salim, der noch immer für Javed arbeitet, lädt Jamal zu sich nach Hause ein, verschweigt ihm jedoch Latikas Aufenthaltsort. Jamal folgt Salim unerkannt zu Javeds Villa, in der er auf Latika trifft, die nun mit Javed zusammenlebt. Er bemerkt, dass Latika gerade *Wer wird Millionär?* im Fernsehen sieht. Jamal versucht, sie davon zu überzeugen, ein neues Leben mit ihm zu beginnen, doch sie scheint gefangen in Javeds Villa. Jamal verspricht ihr, jeden Tag um 17 Uhr am Bahnhof „Victoria Terminus" auf sie zu warten. Eines Tages kommt Latika tatsächlich zum Bahnhof, und Jamal und sie sehen sich, doch Salim und weitere Mitglieder von Javeds Gang fangen Latika ein und bringen sie zurück zu Javed. Durch seinen Job in der Telekommunikationsfirma gelingt es Jamal, Kandidat bei

Wer wird Millionär? zu werden. Latika sieht die Show in Javeds Haus und wird überraschenderweise von Salim gedrängt, zu Jamal zu flüchten. Mit Salims Hilfe gelingt Latika die Flucht. Bevor Jamal, der seine Unschuld auf der Polizeiwache beweisen konnte, die letzte Quizfrage beantwortet, macht er Gebrauch von dem Telefonjoker und ruft vermeintlicherweise Salim an. Da Salim sein Handy jedoch Latika gegeben hat, nimmt sie ab. Zwar weiß sie die richtige Antwort auf die Quizfrage nicht, doch das ist Jamal nicht wichtig. Jamal rät die korrekte Antwort und gewinnt 20 Millionen Rupien, während in Parallelmontage gezeigt wird, wie Salim Javed erschießt und selbst von Javeds Gang erschossen wird. Die letzte Szene zeigt Jamal und Latika, die sich am Bahnhof treffen und nun endlich glücklich vereint sind. Es folgt eine abschließende Tanzszene zu dem Song *Jai Ho*.

Die Personen

Jamal Malik

Jamal K. Malik ist die zentrale Figur des Films, dargestellt im Alter von sieben, 13 und 18 Jahren. Er ist ein Junge aus den Slums von Mumbai. Sein älterer Bruder Salim und er werden im Alter von sieben Jahren Waisen, sodass beide schnell lernen müssen, für sich selbst zu sorgen. Die Brüder lernen Latika, ebenfalls ein Mädchen aus den Slums, kennen und sie nennen sich fortan „The Three Musketeers". Jamal mag Latika sehr gern und wird sich später unsterblich in sie verlieben, wird jedoch zunächst von ihr getrennt. Die Brüder verbringen einen großen Teil ihrer Jugend als Taschendiebe und später als angebliche Fremdenführer im Taj Mahal, wo recht deutlich wird, wie clever Jamal ist. Als Erwachsener arbeitet Jamal als „chai wallah" (Teejunge) in einem Callcenter in Mumbai und versucht stets, seine Jugendliebe Latika wiederzufinden. Er wird schließlich Kandidat bei *Who Wants to Be a Millionaire?*, jedoch nicht in der Absicht reich zu werden, sondern um auf diese Weise Latikas Aufmerksamkeit zu erlangen. Dies zeigt sowohl seinen Optimismus und seine Beharrlichkeit, als auch sein Desinteresse an finanziellem Reichtum. Im Studio erscheint Jamal zunächst schüchtern, reagiert dann jedoch immer schlagfertiger, sowohl gegenüber dem Quizmaster Prem Kumar als auch gegenüber der Polizei, die ihn kurz vor der letzten Quizfrage als Betrüger festnimmt und foltert. Schließlich wird er freigelassen, gewinnt den Hauptpreis und kann endlich mit seiner großen Liebe Latika zusammen sein – eine Entwicklung „from rags to riches".

Salim Malik

Salim ist der ältere Bruder von Jamal, ebenfalls aufgewachsen in den Slums von Mumbai. Er ist Realist und sehr pragmatisch veranlagt, da er schon früh weiß, sein eigenes Geld zu verdienen und Situationen schnell zu durchschauen. Im Wesentlichen erscheint Salim als skrupelloser Krimineller, für den im Leben Geld und Einfluss das Wichtigste sind: Er beraubt und erschießt kaltblütig den Gangster Maman, arbeitet daraufhin für einen weiteren Kriminellen namens Javed und vergewaltigt offensichtlich Latika. Sein Charakter ist widersprüchlich, da er einerseits streng gläubiger Muslim, andererseits Auftragskiller für Javed ist. Gegen Ende des Films findet eine innere Wandlung statt: Salim hilft Latika dabei, Javed zu entkommen und zu Jamal zu gelangen. Dabei opfert er sich für die Liebe zwischen Jamal und Latika, denn er erschießt Javed und wird selbst erschossen.

Latika

Latika, aufgewachsen in den Slums von Mumbai, ist als kleines Kind Waise geworden und hat sich mit Jamal und Salim angefreundet. Sie arbeitet mit ihnen zusammen für den Gangster Maman als Bettlerin und kann ihm, anders als Jamal und Salim, nicht entkommen. Als jungfräuliche Tänzerin bzw. Prostituierte arbeitend wird sie von Jamal und Salim gefunden und befreit, indem Salim ihren Zuhälter Maman erschießt. Später wohnt sie zusammen mit dem Gangsterboss Javed, der sie offensichtlich sehr schlecht behandelt. Gefangen in dieser kriminellen Welt, kann sie nicht mit ihrer eigentlich großen Liebe Jamal zusammenkommen, bis sich schließlich Salim für sie opfert und sie durch seine Hilfe Javed entkommen kann. Latikas Haltung ist tendenziell passiv und konform; sie hat sich allen Männern gefügt, war von ihnen abhängig und hat im Gegensatz zu Jamal kaum für ihre große Liebe gekämpft.

Prem Kumar

Der Quizmaster der Show, Prem Kumar, der sich selbst mühsam aus den Straßen hochgekämpft hat, hegt keine Sympathien für seinen Kandidaten Jamal. Er bezichtigt ihn stattdessen des Betrugs und veranlasst Jamals Festnahme und Folter. Im Studio spielt er seine Überlegenheit Jamal gegenüber stark aus und seine heuchlerische Art wird vor allem deutlich, als er Jamal absichtlich einen falschen Tipp gibt. Er repräsentiert das Motto des Showgeschäfts „Mehr Schein als Sein", denn er beginnt immer dann zu lächeln, zu tanzen und zu klatschen, wenn die Kameras laufen und auf ihn gerichtet sind.

Maman

Der skrupellose Kinderhändler Maman bildet Straßenkinder zu professionellen Bettlern aus, lässt sie für sich arbeiten und nimmt ihnen sogar ihr Augenlicht, damit sie mehr Geld einbringen. Später ist er auch Zuhälter von Latika und verdient an ihr als Tänzerin Geld. Als Jamal und Salim Latika aus seinen Fängen befreien, wird Maman schließlich von Salim erschossen, denn „Maman never forgets" und Salim möchte kein Risiko eingehen.

Javed Khan

Der gierige Gangsterboss Javed lässt Salim als Auftragskiller für ihn arbeiten, nachdem dieser seinen Erzfeind Maman umgebracht hat. Er lebt mit Latika zusammen, misshandelt und vereinnahmt sie, bis er schließlich von Salim in seinem Badezimmer erschossen wird.

Biographical information

Danny Boyle
He directed *Slumdog Millionaire* together with co-director Loveleen Tandan. Born in Manchester, UK in 1956, Boyle won an Academy Award ("Oscar") in the category "Best Achievement in Directing" as well as other awards in 2009 for *Slumdog Millionaire* (2008). The British filmmaker is also well-known for films such as *Trainspotting* (1996), *The Beach* (2000) and *28 Days Later* (2002).

Dev Patel
(Jamal, 18)
Born in London, UK in 1990, Dev Patel is the main protagonist in *Slumdog Millionaire*. Boyle's daughter, a fan of the British TV series *Skins*, recommended Patel for the role. Unlike most famous young Indian actors who are rather the "gym type", Patel was reportedly chosen for *Slumdog Millionaire* due to his "average Joe" appearance. He was nominated for and won a number of awards for his performance in *Slumdog Millionaire*.

Freida Pinto
(Latika, 18)
The former model, Freida Pinto, was born in 1984 in Mumbai (Bombay), India, and had not starred in a feature film before her role in *Slumdog Millionaire*. Pinto, who had only begun to take acting classes when auditioning to play the female lead Latika, was trained in some forms of Indian classical dance and Salsa. She was nominated for and won several awards such as "Best Supporting Actress", "Best Kiss" and "Outstanding Performance".

Madhur Mittal
(Salim, 18)
The Indian actor Madhur Mittal was born in Agra, India, in 1988. In 1997, Mittal won "Boogie Woogie", a popular Indian reality-based dance show. He performed in various stage shows and was a child actor in well-known Hindi films such as *Say Salaam India* (2007). In 2009, Mittal was nominated for the Black Reel Award in the category "Best Ensemble" and won the Screen Actors Guild Award along with the entire cast for their outstanding performance in *Slumdog Millionaire* (2008).

Anil Kapoor
(Prem Kumar)
Born in Maharashtra, India in 1959, the son of film producer Surinder Kapoor plays the game show host in *Slumdog Millionaire*. Initially, Boyle wanted Sharukh Khan, an Indian actor who had hosted the final Indian series of *Who Wants to Be a Millionaire?* to play the role of the game show host. Anil Kapoor joined Roshan Taneja's Acting School and starred as a celebrity guest on the show *Who Wants to Be a Millionaire?* (*Kaun Banega Crorepati*) in 2001. He has played various supporting and leading roles in Indian movies which have earned him several awards and nominations.

Rubina Ali
(Latika, 7)
A child from the Mumbai slums in real life, Rubina Ali, together with Anne Berthod and Divya Dugar, wrote the book *Slumgirl Dreaming – My Journey to the Stars* which was published in 2009 after *Slumdog Millionaire* was released.

Scene index

Based on the original UK-DVD version (*Pathé/Celador Films/Film4, 2008*) with English *WWM* question cards and parts in Hindi.

Scene	Summary	Time
Chapter 1	Jamal is beaten and interrogated by a police officer. Title card appears. Jamal is introduced in the quiz show "Who Wants to Be a Millionaire?" (WWM).	0:00:00
Chapter 2	Second police officer enters, Jamal is tortured. Police officers wonder what Jamal, a "slumdog" could know.	0:03:06
Chapter 3	Flashback: Jamal (7) and his brother Salim play at the airfield with other boys from the slum, and are then chased through slums. At school, they read "The Three Musketeers".	0:05:51
Chapter 4	At the police office: Police officers and Jamal watch video-taped WWM on TV. WWM question on film actor is posed. Flashback: Jamal and Salim make money by renting latrines but Jamal himself is on the toilet. Amitabh Bachchan visits Mumbai. Salim locks Jamal up in latrine. Jamal jumps into excrement in order to meet Bachchan, and gets his signature.	0:09:13
Chapter 5	Police office again: WWM question on the national emblem of India, Jamal does not know the answer and uses a lifeline: Ask the Audience.	0:14:05
Chapter 6	Jamal wins 4000 rupees. The next question is on the god Rama. Flashback: Jamal's mother dies in a Hindu attack on Muslims in the slums. Dissolve from dead mother to police interrogation.	0:15:40
Chapter 7	Jamal and Salim look down on burning slums. Later, they try to sleep in a shed. Latika is outside in the rain. Jamal wants to offer her shelter which Salim half-heartedly accepts.	0:19:54
Chapter 8	WWM: Prem Kumar talking Hindi. The question is on a famous Indian poet. Flashback: Maman takes Jamal, Salim and Latika from the waste dump to his "child beggar camp".	0:22:25
Chapter 9	In the camp, Salim and Arvind practise singing. Children are begging in the streets. Salim is in charge of the other children, bosses them around, threatens to drop baby. Jamal and Latika take revenge and put "chillies on his willy" while Salim is asleep.	0:25:06
Chapter 10	Salim witnesses how Arvind is blinded by Maman and his gang after Arvind has performed as a singer. At the same time, Jamal, preparing for his performance, dances for Latika and they imagine their romantic future together. Salim comes for Jamal and warns him, referring to Athos and Porthos, two of the three musketeers. Salim escapes with Jamal from Maman's camp and Latika follows them. However, only the boys manage to jump on a moving train, as Salim lets go of Latika's hand. She is forced to stay with Maman.	0:28:41
Chapter 11	On the train, the boys make money by selling things. They seem to get along fairly well. ("Paper Planes" song)	0:36:45
Chapter 12	Leap in time: the boys get off the train as 13-year-olds in Agra. They make money at the Taj Mahal: Jamal works as a fake tour guide while Salim robs tourists. Jamal has an encounter with an American couple: When Jamal is beaten up by a police officer, the Americans give him money to show him what the "real America" is like in contrast to the "real India". At night, Jamal enjoys an open air opera while Salim and the others steal from the audience. Jamal thinks of Latika (flashback and flash-forward).	0:39:53

Scene index

Scene	Summary	Time
Chapter 13	The next WWM question is on the American $100 bill. Camera shots from the studio and its production, e.g. backstage, are shown. In the police office, Jamal is asked how he knew what was printed on the Amerian bill, whereas he does not know what is printed on Indian money. Jamal starts explaining: "Bombay had turned into Mumbai …"	0:46:38
Chapter 14	Flashback: Jamal and Salim are back in Mumbai. 'Latika's motif' plays in the scene as Jamal is looking for her in Mumbai. Salim and Jamal work in a restaurant kitchen for a living. Jamal finds blind Arvind and gives him US money which explains how he knew the answer to the WWM question. Arvind tells Jamal about Latika who is now called "Cherry".	0:48:14
Chapter 15	Jamal and Salim look for Latika in the red light district. They find her where she is being trained as a dancer. After Salim kills Maman, they rescue her, take Maman's money and escape (cinematic devices: Jamal's perspective/"subjective camera"). On the show, the next question is on the inventor of the revolver.	0:52:21
Chapter 16	Jamal, Salim and Latika are in a hotel. Salim drinks alcohol. Latika comes out of the shower to get a towel, Jamal is polite and does not look at her. Salim leaves the hotel and looks for Javed in order to work for him. Javed likes Salim because he killed Maman ("my enemy's enemy is a friend").	0:57:31
Chapter 17	Jamal and Latika talk about their relationship ("destiny") in the hotel. Salim comes back and wants to have Latika for himself. He throws Jamal out and threatens him with a revolver. At the police office, Jamal becomes aggressive when one of the police officers offends Latika. The other police officer's reaction: "The slumdog barks …". It becomes obvious that Jamal is only on the show to find Latika.	1:00:14
Chapter 18	Flashback: Jamal (18) works as a chai-wallah in an English-speaking communication company (→ globalization). Jamal replaces a call-centre agent for a second, while the others try to audition for WWM as contestants. At the computer, Jamal tries to find Latika and receives too many results. However, he succeeds in finding Salim and they talk to each other on the phone. On the show, Jamal answers a question on GB which he knew thanks to his job in an English-speaking company.	1:04:24
Chapter 19	Flashback: Jamal meets Salim on an upper storey in a half-constructed building. In a "fantasy scene" Jamal pictures a fight with Salim at the end of which both fall down the building. In reality, Jamal is very mad at Salim who tries to explain the situation. Later, they both look down on "their old" slums: Salim, still working for Javed, feels as if he is "in the centre of the centre" (of India). Salim invites Jamal to his place and tells Jamal that Latika is "gone – long gone".	1:10:22
Chapter 20	At Salim's place, Salim is called (obviously to kill somebody). Jamal watches him pray and follows him to Javed's mansion. Jamal sees Latika there and gets inside by pretending to be a kitchen assistant. Again, Latika's motif is played in the background. Latika is happy at first, then realizes that being with Jamal would not work and becomes afraid because she is with Javed and is going to move soon. WWM is on in the background, but when Javed comes home he switches the program in order to watch a cricket game. Latika throws Jamal out, but he tells her that he will wait for her at the VT station every day at 5 pm. He says "I love you", but she does not respond.	1:13:22
Chapter 21	On the show, a question on cricket is asked. Jamal does not know the answer, but thinks of Latika and goes on playing.	1:21:14

Scene	Summary	Time
Chapter 22	At the train station, Latika and Jamal see each other (origin of recurring shot of Latika). However, she is kidnapped by Salim and Javed's men and Salim's knife cuts her cheek. Jamal is shocked and frustrated.	1:22:06
Chapter 23	Dissolving scenes: On the show, there is a commercial break. In the bathroom, the show's host and Jamal meet. The melody of "O… Saya" comes in ('slum motif') as Prem Kumar indirectly states that he is from the slums. The host talks about destiny and leaves the letter 'B' on the bathroom mirror for Jamal to see. Back in the hot seat, but still in the commercial break, Jamal hears the host say: "From rags to rajah – it's your destiny." Jamal uses his 50:50 lifeline: B and D remain. Jamal answers "D" which is actually right. Prem Kumar is surprised and shocked (gesture/facial expression), but then still manages to fake joy for Jamal's success, dances around and smiles. Jamal, more confident now and expecting the next question, ironically says: "But … maybe it's written, no?" The show is interrupted before the last question, which is to be asked on the next day. The host leads Jamal to the police officers and is convinced that Jamal is a cheat.	1:24:47
Chapter 24	The police officer now knows Jamal's story and believes him because Jamal is a truthful person. Jamal tells the police officer about Latika: There is a flashback of Jamal looking into Javed's mansion which is empty. Latika is watching the news about WWM (and Jamal) in Javed's new house together with other girls and Salim. Javed changes the programme and the girls start dancing. Salim gives Latika the keys to his car and his mobile phone and persuades her to go and find her love. Afterwards, Salim goes into the bathroom while Latika gets into his car and drives to the WWM studio with Salim's mobile on the back seat.	1:32:19
Chapter 25	In a cross-cut: Jamal is set free by the police and is taken back to the WWM studio. Latika is driving to the studio. People recognize Jamal as they have seen him on the show the day before. The final preparations for the WWM show are made. People nation-wide are preparing to watch WWM. Latika gets out of the car because of a traffic jam.	1:36:27
Chapter 26	The final question of the show is on the third name of the three musketeers. Flashbacks of school time and shelter from rain with Latika as the third musketeer are shown. The various parallel settings and actions are depicted in a cross-cut: Jamal in the studio, the audience including Latika in front of their TVs and Salim in the bathroom preparing his death in the bathtub full of money. Jamal chooses the telephone lifeline and Salim's mobile phone starts ringing on the backseat of the car. Latika starts running (→ film poster) and finally gets to the car and picks up the phone. There is a flashback of the first encounter with Latika ("My name is Latika"). Latika is on the phone, does not know the answer but says that she's safe and, in Hindi, "I'm yours". Jamal guesses and wins while at the same time Salim kills Javed and in return is shot, too (Salim's last words: "God is great"). The audience celebrates Jamal's victory.	1:38:51
Chapter 27	At the VT station, Jamal and Latika meet. Latika's motif is played. Flashbacks from their childhood and their youth are shown, and in a rewind mode, the kidnapping sequence is depicted. Jamal and Latika are convinced that "this is our destiny". The title card says "D: It is written".	1:46:10
Chapter 28	There is a dancing scene with the credits in the end.	1:48:42

Vorüberlegungen zum Einsatz des Films im Unterricht

Die Filmanalyse ist inzwischen im Englischunterricht der Oberstufe fest verankert. Dies liegt zum einen daran, dass die Ausbildung von *media literacy* in den Richtlinien und Vorgaben für das Fach Englisch einen großen Stellenwert hat, und zum anderen daran, dass das Medium Film die Schülerinnen und Schüler intrinsisch motiviert und Englischlehrerinnen und -lehrer dieses Potenzial immer häufiger nutzen.

Der mit mehreren Oscars ausgezeichnete Film *Slumdog Millionaire* des britischen Regisseurs Danny Boyle eignet sich aus verschiedenen Gründen für den Einsatz im Englischunterricht in der Oberstufe: Er ist sprachlich interessant, cineastisch anspruchsvoll und nicht zuletzt thematisch aufgrund der durchaus provokativen und umstrittenen Inhalte besonders vielversprechend. *Slumdog Millionaire* bietet vielfältige Anknüpfungspunkte bezüglich der erforderlichen Inhalte in der Oberstufe, insbesondere für das Zentralabitur (z. B. in Nordrhein-Westfalen: *post-colonialism: the post-colonial experience in India; the American Dream – then and now* und *globalisation;* s. unten: „Thematisch"). Somit ist er sehr gut im Rahmen einer Filmanalyse bzw. auch für weitergehende handlungs- und produktionsorientierte Aufgaben geeignet.

Sprachlich

- Wegen der weltweiten Bedeutung des Englischen (*English as lingua franca*) sollten Schülerinnen und Schüler mit verschiedenen Sprachvarietäten und anglophonen Kulturen vertraut gemacht werden. Ein zentrales Ziel des Fremdsprachenunterrichts ist daher die Ausbildung von *intercultural communicative competence.* Dieser Forderung wird im Film dadurch Rechnung getragen, dass in ihm größtenteils die indische Varietät des Englischen benutzt wird und die Schülerinnen und Schüler einen, wenn auch eingeschränkten, Einblick in das Leben und die Kultur Indiens bekommen. In diesem Zusammenhang ist die Tatsache interessant, dass der Regisseur selbst Brite ist und der Zuschauer den Einblick in die indische Kultur (die Co-Regisseurin ist Inderin) somit teilweise auch „durch dessen Brille" bekommt, was weiteren Anlass zur Diskussion bietet.
- Im Film gibt es mehrfach Einschübe in Hindi und entsprechende Untertitel auf Englisch. Hieran kann man sehr gut das linguistische Phänomen des *code-switching* thematisieren und Gründe für den Wechsel analysieren.
- Der Film *Slumdog Millionaire* eignet sich außerdem ausgezeichnet, um die *basic language skills* zu trainieren: Im Film wird die indische Varietät des Englischen benutzt, sodass die Schülerinnen und Schüler das Hörverstehen einer Varietät trainieren können, die nicht der *Received Pronunciation* entspricht. Diese Varietät ist sehr herausfordernd, sodass der Einsatz in der Oberstufe am geeignetsten erscheint. Jedoch sollten die Schülerinnen und Schüler auch frühzeitig darauf hingewiesen werden, dass beim Anschauen eines Films nicht unbedingt jedes Wort verstanden werden muss (*listening for gist*). Die visuelle Filmsprache unterstützt das Verständnis zudem sehr gut. Durch die Spezialeffekte, ebenso wie durch die zwischendurch eingeblendeten englischen Untertitel, wenn Hindi gesprochen wird, ergeben sich außerdem Pausen. Durch diese Untertitel, ebenso wie durch das Einblenden der WWM-Fragen und -Antwortoptionen als *close-ups* wird sogar das Leseverstehen in der Fremdsprache mittrainiert. Die Lesekompetenz spielt jedoch eine noch größere Rolle, wenn man mit den Schülerinnen und Schülern ihrem Sprachniveau entsprechende Zusatzmaterialien zum Film liest (z. B. Buchausschnitte aus *Q & A* von Vikas Swarup, Ausschnitte aus dem Drehbuch von Simon Beaufoy, Hintergrundartikel und Kommentare zum Film). Bezüglich der produktiven Fertigkeiten, Sprechen und Schreiben, provoziert

Slumdog Millionaire aufgrund der kontroversen Inhalte geradezu spontane Reaktionen (*fluency*). Die vielfältigen Inhalte bieten auch interessante Präsentationsthemen für Schülerinnen und Schüler. Die Vielfalt an Themen ermöglicht außerdem eine Vielzahl verschiedener Textsorten, welche die Schülerinnen und Schüler im Rahmen der Behandlung von *Slumdog Millionaire* verfassen können (z. B. *essays, reports, letters*).

Cineastisch
- Schülerinnen und Schüler schauen in ihrer Freizeit gerne Filme, meist jedoch ohne notwendige Sensibilität und Reflektionsfähigkeit. Daher ist es enorm wichtig, dass sie im Unterricht *media literate* werden, also über die Produktion eines Films nachdenken und ein Gespür für die cineastischen Mittel und ihre Wirkungen bekommen. Zudem können sich die Schülerinnen und Schüler über ihre Eindrücke austauschen, weitere Perspektiven kennenlernen und auf diese Weise den Film verarbeiten.
- Der Film *Slumdog Millionaire* bietet viele Möglichkeiten für eine Filmanalyse, da er eine breite Palette filmischer Stilmittel verwendet (z. B. *flashbacks, dissolves, cross-cutting*; Soundtrack mit bestimmten *motifs*; interessante Kameraführung; Spezialeffekte).
- Die Produktionsbedingungen und -hintergründe können miteinbezogen werden, da auf der DVD sehr interessante *extras/special features* mit einer Fülle an Ansatzpunkten für den Unterricht in der Oberstufe vorhanden sind.
- Im Unterricht sollte insbesondere die Darstellung eines TV-Formats innerhalb eines Films (*WWM* innerhalb von *Slumdog Millionaire* – *medium within a medium*) angesprochen und die Wirkung analysiert werden.
- In einer rezeptionsästhetischen Herangehensweise sollte man zudem die Wirkung des Films auf die Schülerinnen und Schüler thematisieren, insbesondere weil die Charaktere ungefähr im gleichen Alter sind wie die Schülerinnen und Schüler und weil bestimmte *universals* behandelt werden (z. B. Freundschaft, Familie und Liebe, aber auch das Verfolgen individueller Ziele). Dadurch werden die meisten Schülerinnen und Schüler vermutlich automatisch mit dem Hauptcharakter und seinen Höhen und Tiefen mitfühlen. Diese emotionale Bindung hat sicherlich einen positiven Einfluss auf die Bereitschaft der Schülerinnen und Schüler, sich mit dem Film auseinanderzusetzen.

Thematisch
- Der Film *Slumdog Millionaire* eignet sich hervorragend, um Einblicke in die indische Kultur und in Themen des Landes zu bekommen (vgl. z. B. zentrale Abiturprüfung 2011 in Hamburg: *Present-day India – A mosaic of contrasts*).
- Im Rahmen einer Unterrichtseinheit zu *post colonialism* kann der Film z. B. unter *The postcolonial experience in India* eingesetzt werden (vgl. z. B. die Abiturthemen für das Jahr 2012 in Nordrhein-Westfalen)
- Der Film stellt Indien aus der Perspektive von Jamal, einem Jungen aus den Slums von Mumbai, dar. Dementsprechend ist das Bild durch viel Brutalität, Armut und Kriminalität gekennzeichnet und sollte somit eher in der Oberstufe behandelt werden (in Deutschland ab 12 Jahren freigegeben, in UK ab 15 Jahren). Das sich durch den Film ziehende Thema von Armut in den Slums und Kriminalität könnte als Aufhänger für *global challenges* im Rahmen des Themas *globalisation* betrachtet und anhand der weltweiten teils positiven Reaktionen und teils harschen Kritik am Film analysiert werden. Ein besonderes Augenmerk kann man hier auf das Wort *Slumdog* und dessen Assoziationen legen.
- Das Leben von Jamal folgt im Verlauf des Films dem Sprichwort „from rags to riches" oder besser „from rags to raja", jedoch in abgewandelter Form zu dem ursprünglichen Konzept. Es besteht daher die Möglichkeit, Parallelen zwischen dem im Film angedeuteten *Indian Dream* und *The American Dream then and now* zu ziehen und Unterschiede herauszuarbeiten.

- Weitere thematisch interessante Punkte sind typische Hollywood- und Bollywood-Aspekte im Film (Farben, Musik, Produktion, etc.) ebenso wie das sich durch den gesamten Film ziehende Thema *destiny*.

Mediale Basis des Unterrichtsmodells ist die britische DVD-Fassung des Films von Regisseur Danny Boyle: *Slumdog Millionaire*, Pathé/Celador Films/Film4 (2008), zu dem Simon Beaufoy das Drehbuch geschrieben hat. Diese UK-DVD Version hat der deutschen Version (2009 erschienen) gegenüber den Vorteil, dass die *Wer Wird Millionär*-Fragetafeln wie im Originalfilm auf Englisch erscheinen, während sie in der deutschen Fassung ins Deutsche übersetzt wurden. Gleiches gilt für die Untertitel, die in den Teilen des Films eingeblendet werden, in denen Hindi gesprochen wird. Außerdem wird in diesem Unterrichtsmodell von dem Audiokommentar des Regisseurs Danny Boyle Gebrauch gemacht (*Component 2*), der nicht Bestandteil der deutschen DVD-Version ist. Als dritter Grund für die Verwendung der britischen Fassung lässt sich anführen, dass die deutsche Version nur deutsche Untertitel verwendet und somit *subtitles* auf Englisch nicht didaktisch genutzt werden könnten. Die Angaben in der Szenenübersicht und in den einzelnen *Components* entsprechen den jeweiligen Anfangs- und Endpunkten der Kapitel auf der UK-DVD. Für Lehrer, die nicht mit der DVD-Version aus UK arbeiten, wurde zur Orientierung der *timecode* der deutschen DVD angegeben, da die Kapiteleinteilungen der beiden DVD-Versionen nicht identisch sind.

Klausuren

Im Folgenden finden sich zwei Klausuren, die man nach der Bearbeitung des Unterrichtsmodells einsetzen kann.

Klausur 1 bezieht sich auf Szene 23 des Films, welche auch in *Component 4* behandelt wird. Während unter Punkt 4.1 ein innerer Monolog von Jamal geschrieben wird, sieht die Aufgabenstellung zu Klausur 1 vor, nach einer Inhaltswiedergabe und einer Auseinandersetzung mit den filmischen Mitteln einen inneren Monolog aus der Perspektive von Prem Kumar zu schreiben. Es empfiehlt sich daher, den gesamten Film gezeigt und die Analyse und Wirkung filmischer Mittel eingeübt zu haben.

Klausur 2 ist ein Essay aus dem *TIME Magazine*. Der Autor lobt den Film *Slumdog Millionaire* und argumentiert gegen negative Kritiken des Films. Er bezieht sich sowohl auf die indische Gesellschaft als auch auf die Geschichte, die der Film erzählt. Der Text eignet sich somit sehr gut, um einen Leserbrief zu schreiben, da verschiedene Themen aufgegriffen und kommentiert bzw. je nach Interesse des Schülers/der Schülerin vertieft werden können.

Während sich **Klausur 1** sowohl für Grund- als auch Leistungskurse eignet, sollte **Klausur 2** aufgrund der Komplexität der Aufgabenstellung und vor allem der Textvorlage eher im Leistungskurs eingesetzt werden.

The bathroom scene: Cinematic devices and Prem Kumar's point of view

DVD *Slumdog Millionaire*, scene 23, in parts (01:24:48–01:26:23)

Assignments

Take your time to read through the tasks of this test. You are going to watch the beginning of scene 23 twice. Take notes while watching. You will then be given 10 minutes between the first and second viewing and can refine your notes in the second viewing.

1. Summarize the main contents of this scene.

2. Describe the cinematic devices Boyle uses in this *bathroom scene* and explain their respective functions.

3. Write a short interior monologue about Prem Kumar's feelings and thoughts at the different stages of this scene. As you are writing from the host's perspective, try to make sure to use his style and appropriate content.

Erwartungshorizont zu Klausur 1

zu 1:
- setting: in the studio's bathroom during a commercial break
- Jamal does not know the answer to the next question; he is frustrated
- Prem talks about his past and how he has become a rich and successful person
- Prem writes letter B on the mirror saying "maybe it's written" in order to trick Jamal
- Jamal sees the letter when washing his hands and looks pensive

zu 2:
- picture of Jamal is shown upside down → reflects his feeling of exasperation: for Jamal, the whole world is turned upside down because he doesn't know the answer and is therefore afraid that he might never see Latika again
- the lighting makes Prem Kumar cast a big shadow → since *to cast a long shadow* stands for having considerable influence on other people or events, this might stand for Prem's power in this situation and his conviction of being able to trick Jamal
- due to the lighting, Prem's face is hardly visible, only outlines → hints at the fact that Prem is hiding something
- *low-angle shot* of Prem while he is urinating and talking about his story of having become a millionaire overnight → makes Prem appear taller and hence emphasizes his power in sharp contrast to Jamal who is cowered down
- the slum motif (*O… Saya*) comes in when Prem talks about his own past → to underline Prem's life *from rags to riches*; this song is played in the context of the slums; Prem is also from the slums and does not want Jamal to write the same story of success
- the way light is shed on Jamal, his face is presented halfway in darkness, halfway in light → he is not *enlightened*; his insecurity is emphasized: he does not know the answer, does not know whether he can trust Prem
- *over-the-shoulder shots* of both Prem and Jamal with their faces visible in the mirror → e.g. to make both perspectives comprehensible for the viewer; both Jamal and Prem reflect about their lives and their situation
- generally: many close-ups → to see Jamal's and Prem's facial expressions better and thus to be able to guess, like a detective, whether Prem is telling the truth and whether Jamal is going to trust him or not

zu 3: The students' anwers will vary here. However, the style is likely to be a *stream-of-consciousness* style of writing including many personal thoughts and feelings. Some content-related aspects that might show up in students' answers, as they have already seen the continuation of the film at that stage:
- Prem thinks about his past and how he has become so successful
- he does not want anybody to take this unique career away from him and sees Jamal as his rival
- he is under the producers' pressure; they expect Jamal to lose
- he thinks about how he could best feed Jamal the wrong answer
- in his eyes, Jamal is a cheat
- he expects Jamal to take the bait

Jyoti Thottam: The Oscar goes to … India – for inspiring a film that reveals what's truly incredible about the country and its people

My favorite scene in *Slumdog Millionaire* comes toward the end, in the tense battle of wits between the supercilious game-show host, Prem, and the hero, Jamal. Prem expects Jamal to lose, and when he doesn't, assumes that he's cheating. Once Prem realizes that a kid from the slums might win – fairly – he angrily tosses him off to a waiting police
5 van. "It's my show," he says. In two tight shots, with just a few lines of dialogue, the film manages to capture the ambivalence and, sometimes, anger that Indians often direct at those who don't stick to the script.

Watching the arc of *Slumdog Millionaire's* reception in India – it has moved speedily from obscurity to minor phenom to backlash to major phenom and now backlash again
10 – I thought of all those indignant Indians denouncing the film as real-life versions of Prem the game-show host. India spent several years, and millions of dollars, promoting the story of "Incredible India," a shiny new world of prosperity, innovation and opportunity. That world certainly exists for millions of Indians, and for a while it was nice to believe that the lucky inhabitants of "rising India" would somehow lift up the
15 other 900 million. It isn't quite happening that way, as most Indians are well aware, and the rest of the world is wising up. The story that the world is more interested in now is the one told by *Slumdog Millionaire* – the ugliness behind the glittering façade – and that's upsetting. The world is not following the script.

And so the self-proclaimed defenders of India's image have spent the past few weeks
20 reciting what has become a rather predictable litany of sins committed by the film – that it is voyeuristic "poverty porn," that it is implausible and hackneyed, that it's a Western vision of India in which there is nothing but misery, filth and violence. (Aravind Adiga's *The White Tiger*, which won last year's Man Booker literary prize, generated a similar round of complaints.)
25 It's all getting a little, well, implausible and hackneyed. Sandipan Deb, writing in the daily newspaper the *Indian Express* on the morning after the Oscars, insisted that despite the awards for composer A.R. Rahman, sound mixer Resul Pookutty and lyricist Gulzar, the film is still a "Western" film, made by a British director and financed by a British producer. "It's a non-Indian film which happened to have an all-Indian cast," he wrote.
30 This is missing the point. Danny Boyle could not have made the film that he did without this cast and crew, and to pretend otherwise is to belittle their contribution. These Oscars ought to be seen as a validation of everyone who made *Slumdog* possible, particularly Rahman, who might finally take his place among the great film composers of any era or continent. As Pookutty said to the Oscar audience when accepting his statu-
35 ette: "This is not just a sound award; this is history being handed over to me." Drawing the easy distinction between the Indian and non-Indian cast also ignores the way many artists in India actually work. Their world is the world – not just India – and they proudly learn, borrow and are influenced by everything around them. That was obvious in the Japanese taiko drummers pounding behind Rahman on his Oscar-nominated
40 song "O… Saya." And anyone who noticed Irrfan Khan as Jamal's interrogator ought to have a look at his other, much more substantial role in *A Mighty Heart*, playing a Pakistani police captain opposite an American superstar in a British film.

The influence goes both ways. *Slumdog*, which is based on a novel by Indian diplomat Vikas Swarup, approaches India and Indians with a new sensibility. *Slumdog's* central
45 trio aren't victims; they're individuals, and they each manage in different ways to rewrite the lives they've been born into. Jamal, in the film, talks a lot about destiny, but his story is really an argument against it. It's a long way from *City of Joy*, the 1992 film in which Om Puri's noble rickshaw puller shows Patrick Swayze's disillusioned doctor

---

stick to sth to hold fast or adhere resolutely
arc a continuous progression or line of development
obscurity the state of not being well-known
phenom phenomenon
backlash a strong adverse reaction
indignant having or showing angry surprise because one believes that one has been treated unfairly
to denounce to criticize strongly and publicly sb/sth that one thinks is wrong, illegal, etc.
to wise up to become informed or knowledgeable
hackneyed lacking in freshness or originality
filth disgusting dirt
Aravind Adiga an Indian journalist and author

to belittle to cause sb or sth to seem little or less
validation to validate: to prove that sth is true or correct
taiko Japanese drums
to pound to hit sth with repeated heavy blows; to beat heavily
interrogator a person who questions sb closely or aggressively and for a long time

A Mighty Heart a 2007 film directed by Michael Winterbottom

to approach to start dealing with sth in a particular way

the path to enlightenment. *Slumdog* recognizes that poverty isn't ennobling; it's infuriating, and only the cunning escape.

Of course, *Slumdog Millionaire* is not the first to discover this other, more complicated India, as the film's critics correctly point out. It's real for the hundreds of millions of Indians who live in it, the thousands of social workers, nonprofit groups and civil servants who are trying to change it, and those who tell its stories. That includes a handful of young Indian filmmakers who are making movies that are as sharp, challenging and entertaining as the best of Hollywood, although few have been distributed outside India. Let's hope the rest of the world will soon have a chance to see them. It's now their show.

Time, March 9, 2009, p. 52

ennobling tending to exalt
infuriating causing anger and annoyance
cunning clever at deceiving people; characterized by wiliness and trickery

sharp keen in intellect; intellectually penetrating

Assignments

1. Summarize the writer's thoughts on the film and on the reactions to it.
2. In how far do the structure and stylistic devices emphasize these thoughts?
3. Write a letter to the editor in which you discuss the writer's opinion.

Erwartungshorizont zu Klausur 2

zu 1: The writer …
- likes the film
- connects topics of the film to what he thinks is typical of India and its society
- states that film looks beyond the surface (l. 17 "the ugliness behind the glittering façade")
- defends the film against criticism and provides arguments which support his view (e.g. emphasizes that the cast and crew are both Indian and non-Indian and thus it is not a 'Western' film)
- stresses the way in which many Indian artists are influenced by international processes (l. 37: "Their world is the world – not just India")
- provides references to books and other films
- hopes that Indian filmmakers will soon show the world that their films are comparable to the best films of Hollywood
- considers *Slumdog Millionaire* and its success to be a chance for India

zu 2: The writer …
- begins his essay with one film scene which draws the reader (who has seen the film) into the text right away
- repeats certain words/phrases (e.g. show: l. 5, l. 58; script: l. 7, l. 18) and thus connects film and reality
- is ironic when he refers to the criticism of the film (l. 25: "It's all getting a little, well, implausible and hackneyed") as he picks up the words the critics use themselves (l. 21)
- invalidates a critic's argument by first repeating the argument (ll. 25 ff.) and then proving that it is wrong (ll. 30 ff.)

zu 3: Der folgende Leserbrief stellt ein Beispiel dar, wie ein *letter to the editor* verfasst werden könnte. Selbstverständlich sind auch nicht zustimmende Leserbriefe möglich, die den Artikel oder Teile des Artikels kritisieren. Es ist darauf zu achten, dass die Schülerinnen und Schüler mit dem Layout eines Leserbriefes und den formalen Anforderungen vertraut sind.

date

Dear Sir or Madam

I refer to your article on *Slumdog Millionaire* (TIME, March 9). I absolutely agree with the writer's opinion that the film goes beyond the surface and reveals that India's prosperity is not true for the majority of the population. Moreover, I would like to point out that this movie has made me think of India and its people in a way no tourism campaign could have done.

However, I would like to stress that the movie is still a fictive story. This also contradicts some critics' opinion that the film is "implausible and hackneyed". In a feature film, everything is possible – otherwise, it would be called a documentary. Although the movie refers to incidents which might have happened in a similar way in reality, it is a modern fairytale which allows the viewer to escape from reality and start dreaming. The movie is not only about poverty and ugliness; it is also about hope and optimism. I am sure readers will agree with me when I say that this has also contributed to the movie's success. A good movie does not necessarily have to refer to reality – instead, it has to be entertaining and make you think about the story, no matter whether it is implausible and unrealistic or evident and authentic.

Emma Müller, Dortmund

Konzeption des Unterrichtsmodells

Die in den **Vorüberlegungen zum Einsatz des Films** genannten sprachlichen, cineastischen und thematischen Anknüpfungspunkte werden in den folgenden *Components* aufgegriffen und umgesetzt. Die Struktur der einzelnen *Components* folgt immer dem Schema *1. Content, 2. Background, 3. Film analysis,* um möglichst alle relevanten Inhalte und Hintergründe des Films und der Filmanalyse abzudecken. Dieses Unterrichtsmodell dient als Anregung und Pool für vielfältige Ideen zum Umgang mit dem Film *Slumdog Millionaire*. Es wird ausdrücklich darauf hingewiesen, dass nicht alle Aufgaben verwendet werden müssen, sondern ein selektives Vorgehen je nach zur Verfügung stehender Zeit und nach Neigung der Lerngruppe sinnvoll ist. Außerdem sei an dieser Stelle angemerkt, dass das Unterrichtsmodell einige *Weblinks* enthält, deren Aktualität vor dem Unterrichtseinsatz unbedingt überprüft werden sollte. [Stand: Februar 2010]

Component 1 bietet einen Einstieg in den Film, zunächst anhand einer *pre-viewing activity* zum Filmplakat. Daraufhin werden sechs arbeitsteilig zu bearbeitende *long-term while-viewing tasks* vorgeschlagen, welche über den gesamten Film hinweg bearbeitet werden können. Sollte diese Option nicht gewählt werden, bieten die Aufgaben in den anderen *Components* ausreichend Möglichkeit zur Vertiefung. Des Weiteren findet sich in diesem *Component* eine Aufgabe zum Vergleich von Roman (*Q & A*) und Film, zum Begriff „Slumdog" und zu den cineastischen Mitteln während der „slum chase".

Im Rahmen von *Component 2* setzen sich die Schülerinnen und Schüler inhaltlich mit den drei Hauptfiguren Jamal, Salim und Latika sowie mit deren Beziehung auseinander (wichtig, wenn die *long-term while-viewing tasks* nicht behandelt werden). Sie bearbeiten als landeskundlichen Einschub außerdem den religiösen und politischen Hintergrund in Indien in Verbindung mit einer Filmanalyse anhand des Audiokommentars von Danny Boyle.

In *Component 3* wird vorgeschlagen, dass die Schülerinnen und Schüler anhand einer *while-viewing*-Aufgabe zum *listening for detail* motiviert werden, dass sie sich im Rahmen einer Internetrecherche mit den Großstädten Agra und Mumbai auseinandersetzen und sich filmanalytisch mit der Darstellungsform des für den Film besonders interessanten *subjective viewpoint* beschäftigen.

Innerhalb von *Component 4* wird das Verfassen eines inneren Monologs von Jamal zu der Szene vorgeschlagen, in welcher ihm der Gastgeber der Show eine falsche Antwort vorgeben möchte. Diese Bearbeitung wird ausdrücklich empfohlen, wenn man Klausur 1 benutzen möchte. Zum Hintergrund bietet sich, auch in Hinblick auf abiturrelevante Inhalte, die Behandlung des Themas Globalisierung an. Um die Schülerinnen und Schüler im Umgang mit filmischen Mitteln und ihren Effekten zu schulen, können sie außerdem ein True/False-Arbeitsblatt hierzu ausfüllen.

Component 5 vertieft die im Film bedeutsamen Aspekte Geld, Liebe und Schicksal, geht auf den kreativen Umgang mit dem am Ende eingespielten Filmsong *Jai Ho* ein und analysiert zentrale filmische Darstellungsmittel der letzten Kapitel.

Im Rahmen von *Component 6* werden mögliche *post-viewing activities* bearbeitet. Es ist sinnvoll, zunächst die Ergebnisse der *long-term while-viewing tasks* präsentieren zu lassen, wenn diese bearbeitet wurden. Daraufhin könnte man als alternative Verständniskontrolle ein Quiz zum Film im *WWM*-Format durchführen und schließlich eine Filmkritik kommentieren und eine eigene verfassen lassen.

Component 1

Introducing a Slumdog's life

1.1 Pre-viewing activity: Film poster

Als motivierender Einstieg in die Unterrichtseinheit zu *Slumdog Millionaire* bietet sich eine *pre-viewing activity* mithilfe des Filmplakats an (s. *Getting started*, S. 3; in Farbe: www.impawards.com/2008/slumdog_millionaire_xlg.html). Vor dem ersten Ansehen des Films wird das Plakat als Anregung genommen, Vermutungen über den Inhalt des Films anzustellen. Die Ideen könnte der Lehrer/die Lehrerin in Form einer Mind-Map an der Tafel festhalten. In dieser Phase müssten sich diejenigen Schülerinnen und Schüler, die den Film bereits gesehen haben, bei den Spekulationen zurückhalten. Sie könnten in der Zeit z. B. Protokollaufgaben übernehmen, auf die man am Ende der Unterrichtseinheit zurückgreifen kann. Frage 3, die sich eher mit Wirkung und Werbewirksamkeit des Plakats auseinandersetzt, könnte jedoch auch von diesen Schülerinnen und Schülern behandelt werden.
Die folgende Impulsfrage dient einem ersten Brainstorming:

 Have a look at the film poster. What do you expect the film to be about?

- the man in the picture is mean; the woman is running away from him
- a love story; somebody looking for his/her lost love
- quiz format; millionaire; money plays a role; questions and answers might be important

Für eine detailliertere Auseinandersetzung mit dem Plakat:

1. Which genre might this film belong to and why?

   - romantic comedy; action film; drama

2. Have a closer look at the way the two people on the poster are depicted. What might their relationship be like?

   - he isn't looking in her direction, she is running away from him: they are enemies
   - she is thinking about and running towards him: she loves him
   - they are a couple, but might have problems (e.g. with money)

3. Which elements stand out and what might their possible effect be?

   - title *Slumdog Millionaire*: a contradiction in terms/oxymoron
   - very colourful: colours (esp. yellow, purple) create a dramatic effect
   - quiz format of *Who Wants to Be a Millionaire?* → the viewer feels addressed because of question

- Danny Boyle as director is mentioned: way to reach Boyle's fans
- two quotations praising the film: convince audience to watch the movie

Eine alternative *pre-viewing activity* ist die Betrachtung des Filmtrailers, den man unter den „*Special Features*" der DVD finden kann. Mögliche Fragestellungen wären hier:

- What do you expect the film to be about?
- Which key elements of the film are emphasized?
- What might the final outcome of the film be?

In diesem Unterrichtsmodell wird der Trailer als *post-viewing activity* (**Component 6**) behandelt.

1.2 Long-term while-viewing tasks

Dieses Unterrichtsmodell sieht vor, den Film *Slumdog Millionaire* innerhalb von fünf aufeinanderfolgenden *viewing sessions* zu behandeln, welche der Kapiteleinteilung der ersten 5 *Components* entsprechen. Daher könnten *long-term while-viewing tasks* verteilt werden, die zwar im Rahmen der Unterrichtsreihe nicht obligatorisch sind, jedoch sicherstellen, dass der Gesamteindruck des Films nicht verloren geht und der Überblick über die narrative Chronologie, die dem Film zugrunde liegt, gewahrt wird. Folgende sechs Aufgaben könnten dabei arbeitsteilig in sechs verschiedenen Gruppen bearbeitet werden: Darstellung und Entwicklung von vier besonders relevanten Charakteren des Films, Zeitleiste von Jamals Leben sowie Einsatz und Wirkung von Musik und weiteren auditiven Elementen.

1. Development of Jamal's character
2. Development of Salim's character
3. Development of Latika's character
4. Development of Prem Kumar's character
5. Timeline of Jamal's life
6. Music & sound – possible effects

Die Schülerinnen und Schüler sollten vor Beginn des Films selbst wählen, zu welchem Themenschwerpunkt sie im Laufe des Films zum Experten/zur Expertin werden möchten. Neben dieser Interessendifferenzierung gibt es auch eine Leistungsdifferenzierung, da die oben aufgeführten Aufgaben unterschiedlich komplex sind, z. B. ist 1 wesentlich umfangreicher als 3 und 4, 5 und 6 spricht andere Lerntypen an als 1 – 4. Selbstverständlich bietet es sich an, abhängig von der Klassengröße die Anzahl der Gruppen zu reduzieren und z. B. Prem Kumar auszusparen.

Da die Kenntnis der Hauptfiguren zu diesem Zeitpunkt noch nicht vorausgesetzt werden kann, eignet sich *Copy 1* (als OHP-Folie) zur ersten Vorstellung der Charaktere für die Gruppen 1 – 4.

Gruppe 5 erhält als Hilfestellung auf ihrem *Worksheet* (*Copy 3*) eine Blanko-Landkarte von Indien, in welche die verschiedenen Stationen im Leben von Jamal eingetragen werden können. Dazu müssten die Schülerinnen und Schüler zunächst recherchieren, wo sich die Orte Mumbai und Agra befinden, in denen die „Reise" von Jamal und Salim hauptsächlich stattfindet. Die Schülerinnen und Schüler könnten im Anschluss z. B. zu Agra „at age 13, works as tour guide in the Taj Mahal" schreiben und einen Pfeil nach Mumbai zeichnen (s. Lösungsvorschläge zu *while-viewing task 5*). Zusätzlich zur eigentlichen Aufgabe, die zeitliche Abfolge der Ereignisse im Leben von Jamal zu erfassen, könnte Gruppe 5 eine Verbindung zum Thema Landeskunde herstellen, indem sie weitere Informationen zu den Städten (z. B. Einwohnerzahl, Taj Mahal etc.) sammelt.

Die *Worksheets* für die *while-viewing tasks* (**Copies 2–4**) sollten während des gesamten Films ausgefüllt/bearbeitet und deswegen zu jeder *viewing session* mitgebracht werden. Es empfiehlt sich, den Schülerinnen und Schülern im Anschluss an jede Filmvorführung ca. 5 Minuten zur Ergänzung und zum Austausch in Gruppen zu gewähren. Dies ist besonders im Hinblick auf die Präsentation der Ergebnisse im Anschluss an das Anschauen des gesamten Films wichtig (s. *Component 6*). Mögliche Ergebnisse der *long-term while-viewing tasks* werden hinter den **Copies 1–4** vorgestellt.

Jamal

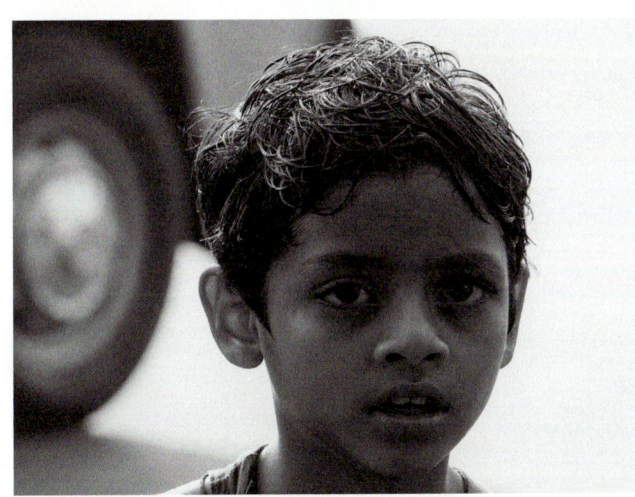 

Salim · Prem Kumar

Latika

Long-term while-viewing tasks: Characters

How is _____ **represented** throughout the film? In what way does he/she **develop** in the course of the film?

Fill in the following grids **while watching** the film step by step. You will have approx. 5 minutes after each viewing session to exchange your findings with your group members and to write down additional information. Pay special attention to the following questions:

Does the representation of _____ **differ from** what you have noted after your last viewing session? If so, in what way?

In how far do **cinematic devices** shape or influence your impression of the character?

This procedure will help you to give a short presentation on the character to your classmates after having watched the whole film.

Viewing session 1:

When (age/stage in life)?	Where (place)?	What (action)?	How (representation, cinematic devices)?

Viewing session 2:

When (age/stage in life)?	Where (place)?	What (action)?	How (representation, cinematic devices)?

Viewing session 3:

When (age/stage in life)?	Where (place)?	What (action)?	How (representation, cinematic devices)?

Viewing session 4:

When (age/stage in life)?	Where (place)?	What (action)?	How (representation, cinematic devices)?

Viewing session 5:

When (age/stage in life)?	Where (place)?	What (action)?	How (representation, cinematic devices)?

Long-term while-viewing task: Timeline of Jamal's life

Timeline with respective stages in Jamal's life:

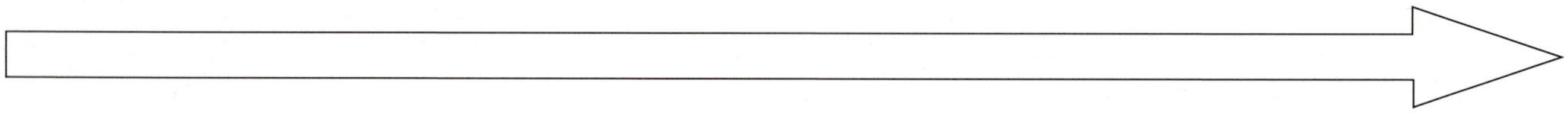

1. With the help of the following map, reconstruct Jamal's journey through the country and his stages in life in the respective cities.

2. After having watched the whole film, there will be a presentation session in class. Be prepared to give a short presentation on the film's underlying chronology based on the stages in Jamal's life. Pay special attention to the use of flashbacks and flash-forwards.

Long-term while-viewing task: Music & sound – possible effects

Listen carefully while watching the film to find out about the relationship between visual and auditory elements. Which songs and sounds do you come across? Are there any recurring themes or motifs you notice throughout the film? In what instances or in connection with which character are they used? Most importantly: What are some possible effects of the soundtrack?

Please fill in the following grids **while watching** the film step by step. You will have approx. 5 minutes after each viewing session to exchange your findings with your group members and to write down additional information.

This procedure will help you to give a short presentation on the film's soundtrack and its effects to your classmates after having watched the whole film.

Viewing session 1:

What (song/sound/motif)?	When (situation)?	Possible effects?

Viewing session 2:

What (song/sound/motif)?	When (situation)?	Possible effects?

Viewing session 3:

What (song/sound/motif)?	When (situation)?	Possible effects?

Viewing session 4:

What (song/sound/motif)?	When (situation)?	Possible effects?

Viewing session 5:

What (song/sound/motif)?	When (situation)?	Possible effects?

Mögliche Ergebnisse der *long-term while-viewing tasks*

Die folgenden möglichen inhaltlichen Ergebnisse sollen keine Musterlösungen sein, sondern stellen erwartbare Schülerantworten zusammenfassend dar und dienen der Lehrperson als Orientierung. Zu *Copy 3* wird ein mögliches Ergebnis geliefert, wie die *map* zu *Jamal's life* ausgefüllt werden könnte.

1. Development of Jamal's character

As a 7-year-old: friendly and polite towards Latika (offers her shelter, makes her laugh); ambitious yet naive (believes he can start a career as a singer when working for Maman); clever (makes money on the train, together with Salim)

As a 13-year-old: intelligent (pretends to be a tour guide, knows how to make money); still in love with Latika, thinks about her all the time; hopeful and even a bit of a dreamer (does not give up trying to find Latika); romantic, believes in destiny (Latika and Jamal talk about their relationship); still a child in contrast to Salim (Salim kills Maman → Jamal is shocked; Salim wants to have Latika for himself whereas Jamal is almost embarrassed and looks away when Latika comes out of the shower)

As an 18-year-old: smart and clever (on the show: remembers incidents in his life in order to answer the questions correctly); acts cool but at the same time is really distracted by his memories; possesses knowledge of human nature (does not trust the host); brave (does not follow Prem's hint); strong/a fighter (survives torture); sarcastic/ironic (towards policemen and Prem); trustworthy/truthful (tells policemen the truth); can keep his feelings under control but when policeman offends Latika, he reacts aggressively; takes the risk to answer the last question because now he knows that Latika is safe; he is not interested in money: even when he wins 20 million rupees, the money is secondary to him – all that matters to him is Latika
→ Jamal is presented as an intelligent, unselfish and hopeful, dreamy character whose only aim is to be with the love of his life, Latika.

2. Development of Salim's character

As a 7-year-old: cunning (e.g. sells autograph → importance of money); protects and takes care of Jamal, but at the same time dominates him/plays the boss; recognizes danger (Maman and his men) and rescues Jamal from being hurt by Maman; clever (makes money on the train, together with Jamal)

As a 13-year-old: criminal (robs tourists); back in Mumbai: pragmatic/realistic; supports his brother in rescuing Latika from Maman; cold-blooded (kills Maman); brave (asking Javed for a job); aggressive and dominating (throws Jamal out, even threatens him with a revolver in order to have Latika for himself)

As an 18-year-old: wants to reunite with Jamal when his brother calls him; cannot understand that Jamal is still in love with Latika; feels very important and influential ("in the centre of the centre"); ruthless (works as a killer for Javed); seems to have a strong religious belief (praying); hurts his brother emotionally (catches Latika in order to bring her back to Javed when she tries to escape and meet with Jamal);

at the end, he shows his brotherly love and helps Latika to run away (he finally realizes how hard Jamal is trying to be with Latika and that they belong together → epiphany); sacrifices himself for the love of Latika and Jamal when he kills Javed and is killed in return; money and religion are important to him (bathtub filled with money, last words: 'God is great')

→ Throughout the film, Salim is interested in money and power. He is a contradictory character who both cares about and emotionally hurts his brother; he is egocentric and yet sacrifices himself for Jamal and Latika.

3. Development of Latika's character

As a 7-year-old: seems to be dependent on Salim and Jamal (is offered shelter); obviously gets along with Jamal very well (soulmates); is presented as a passive victim (e.g. Salim lets go of her hand when they escape from Maman); separated from Jamal

As a 13-year-old: still dependent on others (Maman, when being trained as a dancer in a brothel; rescued by Salim and Jamal); appreciates Jamal's politeness ("you're a sweet boy Jamal"); believes in destiny; submits herself to Salim when he threatens Jamal with a revolver

As an 18-year-old: passive and compliant (towards Javed); obviously scared of Javed; at first does not seem to believe in destiny anymore (does not respond to Jamal's "I love you"); the only time she actively attempts to influence the course of her life is when she tries to escape and meet Jamal at the VT station; suspicious (at first does not trust Salim when he offers her his car key); lacks self-determination (does not organize her escape herself but Salim convinces her to flee); at the end, shows more emotion (happy to hear Jamal's voice, loves him, says in Hindi "I'm yours")

→ Throughout the film, Latika is depicted as a passive victim who is dependent on others and accepts her fate. This is due to the fact that she was never truly independent, and that different men (Maman and Javed, but also Salim) have dominated her all her life.

4. Development of Prem Kumar's character

Not a likeable character: From the beginning, he has an arrogant way of speaking and behaving, e.g. he makes fun of Jamal ("chai wallah"). He is hypocritical, smiles and dances as long as the cameras are on (after all, he is the show's host), but behind his façade he is malicious (gives Jamal a wrong hint and hands him over to the police). He seems to begrudge Jamal's success ("It's my show!") and does not trust him.

5. Timeline of Jamal's life

Die Ereignisse in Jamals Leben beziehen sich auf die in der Show gestellten Quizfragen. Die Schülerinnen und Schüler werden daher vermutlich die Kernaussagen der Quizfragen wiedergeben, um die zeitliche Abfolge der Geschichte zu rekonstruieren und Zusammenhänge herzustellen. Die Fragen, wie sie wortwörtlich im Film gestellt werden, sind im Folgenden dargestellt und dienen lediglich der Orientierung für die Lehrperson.

Question 1: 'Who was the star of the 1973 hit film, Zanjeer?' – Flashback to childhood in a slum in Mumbai (map): 7-year-old Jamal jumping into excrements; getting an autograph from Amitabh Bachchan, an actor → correct answer.

Question 2: 'A picture of three lions is seen in the national emblem of India. What is written underneath it?' – Jamal uses a lifeline and asks the audience.

Question 3: 'In depictions of God Rama, he is famously holding what in his right hand?' – Flashback to Hindu attack on Muslim slum in which Jamal's mother is killed and he sees God Rama almost as a hallucination.

Question 4: 'The song "Darshan Do Ghanshyam" was written by which famous Indian poet?' – Flashback to waste dump and time in Maman's camp in which children have to practise singing in order to work as beggars. The boys manage to escape and get on a train which takes them from Mumbai to Agra (map). In this flashback, there is also a leap in time which means that when the boys arrive in Agra, they are 13 years old. They make money at the Taj Majal in Agra (map).

Question 5: 'On an American hundred dollar bill, there is a portrait of which American statesman?' – Flashback to search for Latika in Mumbai (map). Jamal meets blind Arvind who tells him where to find Latika and knows that Benjamin Franklin is on the American note which Jamal gives him.

Question 6: 'Who invented the revolver?' – Flashback to Salim, Jamal and Latika as 13-year-olds in the hotel room where Salim throws Jamal out by threatening him with a revolver. Flash-forward to interrogation at the police office; flashback to Jamal working as a call centre assistant in an English-speaking company in Mumbai (map), which allows him to answer question 7.

Question 7: 'Cambridge Circus is in which UK city?' – Flashback to Jamal meeting Salim; sees Latika in Javed's mansion.

Question 8: 'Which cricketer has scored the most first centuries in history?' – Flashback to Latika and Jamal trying to meet at the VT station in Mumbai (map) where Javed's men including Salim catch her. Flash-forward to show (bathroom scene). The last question will be posed the next day, and after the show, Prem Kumar leads Jamal to the police, accusing him of cheating. Present time: policeman believes Jamal's story, so he is allowed to answer the last question.

Question 9: 'In Alexander Dumas' book, "The Three Musketeers", two of the musketeers are called Athos and Porthos. What was the name of the third musketeer?' – Present time: In the *WWM* studios in Mumbai (map), Jamal uses his last lifeline, guesses and wins 20 million rupees; he is reunited with Latika at the VT station in Mumbai (map).

Component 1: Introducing a Slumdog's life

> Im Folgenden wird ein mögliches Ergebnis dargestellt, wie die Schülerinnen und Schüler der Gruppe 5 die Karte ausfüllen könnten.

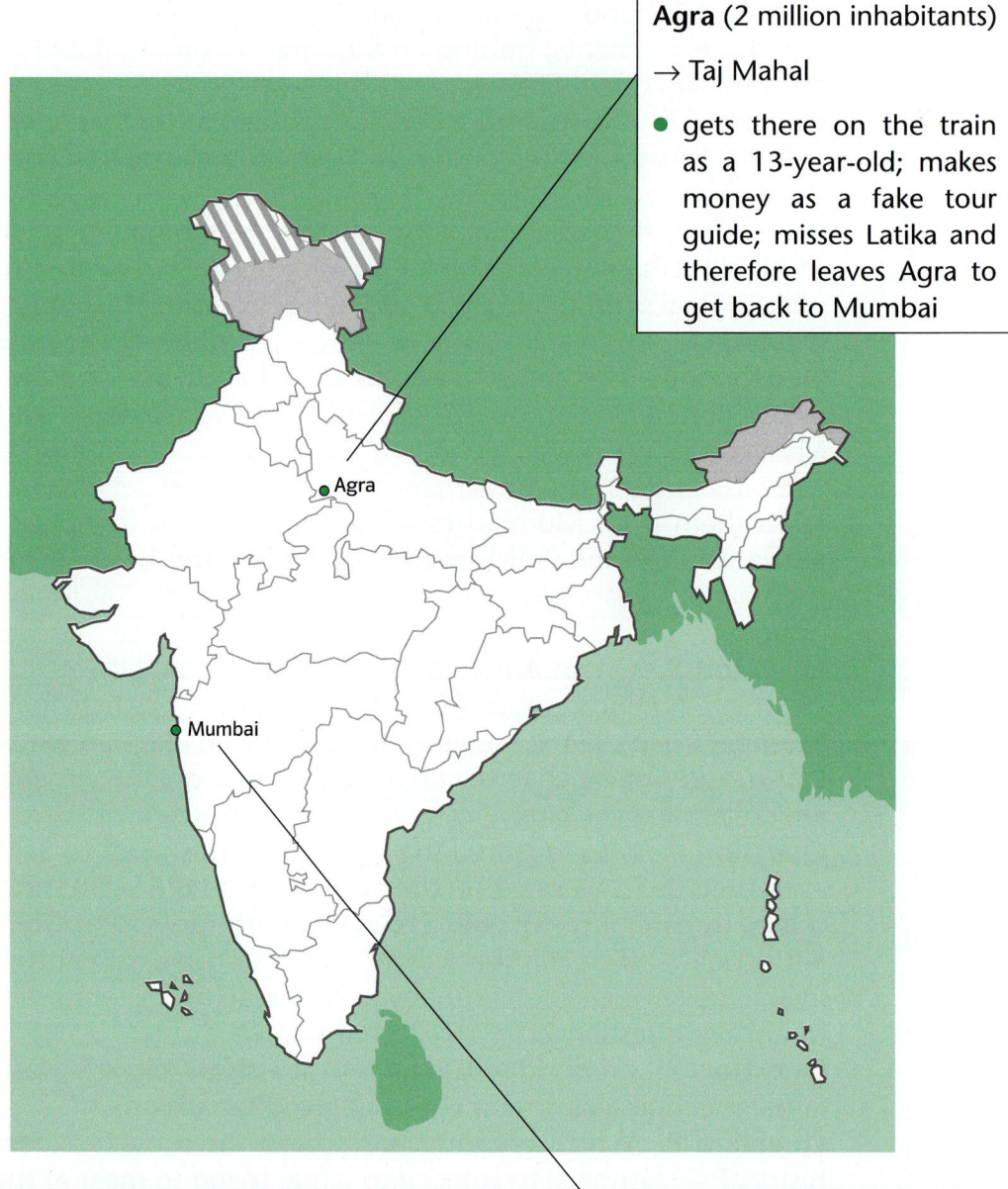

Agra (2 million inhabitants)

→ Taj Mahal

- gets there on the train as a 13-year-old; makes money as a fake tour guide; misses Latika and therefore leaves Agra to get back to Mumbai

Mumbai (12 million inhabitants)

- childhood: slum
- Maman's camp
- leaves Mumbai on the train to Agra as a 7-year-old
- gets back to Mumbai as a 13-year-old
- works in a restaurant kitchen; searches for and finds Latika but is separated from her again because of Salim
- as an 18-year-old:
  works as a call centre assistant in an English-speaking company
  meets with Salim; finds Latika; meets Latika at the VT station; participates in the show *WWM*; finally reunited with Latika at the VT station

From Mumbai to Agra by train (the total distance is more than one thousand kilometres): Jamal and Salim make money on the train by selling things to the passengers.

6. Music & sound – possible effects

Songs/themes are used repeatedly for specific characters and/or situations:

- "Latika's motif" is used when Jamal meets Latika in front of Javed's mansion, or when they meet at the VT station.
- "O… Saya" is used in connection to the slum, e.g. at the very beginning in the slum chase and when Prem Kumar and Jamal talk about their origin in the bathroom scene.

"Jai Ho" is used in the dancing scene at the very end which underlines the happy atmosphere.
"Paper planes" (happy music) is used when the brothers really seem to get along well on the train from Mumbai to Agra.
Generally, drums and fast music are used to underline danger.
→ Music helps the viewer to understand the characters' feelings and/or makes the atmosphere clearer.

1.3 Content: *Who Wants to Be a Millionaire?* – novel into film

Der Film *Slumdog Millionaire* basiert auf dem Roman *Q & A* von Vikas Swarup. Um Unterschiede zwischen den Textsorten kennenzulernen, bietet es sich an, die Darstellungen und Wirkungen einer Roman- und einer Filmszene miteinander zu vergleichen. Dazu eignet sich die Szene, in der Jamal (im Roman *Ram Mohammad Thomas*, der aus der Ich-Perspektive erzählt) zu Beginn der Show *Wer wird Millionär?* vorgestellt wird.
Nachdem der Romanauszug (*Copy 5*) von den Schülerinnen und Schülern als Hausaufgabe vorbereitet wurde, könnte im Unterricht die folgende Filmszene zweimal gezeigt werden: 0:0:57–0:03:06 (Beginn der Szene: Geräusch einer tickenden Uhr (WWM motif); Prem Kumar: "Good evening …"; Ende der Szene: Einstellung von Latika).
Das erste Mal könnten die Schülerinnen und Schüler die Szene unter folgender Fragestellung betrachten:

> How is the TV show presented in the film?
>
> - very similar to the German version (*Wer wird Millionär?*)
> - from the point of view of the contestant (Jamal)
> - production-side/backstage area of the show is presented
> - parallel action/cross-cutting between TV show and interrogation/torture

Vor dem zweiten Ansehen der Szene könnte ein Arbeitsauftrag erteilt werden, in dem die Schülerinnen und Schüler Gemeinsamkeiten und Unterschiede (z.B. in Form einer Tabelle; Vorschlag dazu s.u.) in Partnerarbeit herausarbeiten sollen:

> In pairs, find out the major similarities and differences between the novel excerpt and the film scene. Pay special attention to the following aspects: content, perspective, and realization. Afterwards, try to determine the respective effects which the novel excerpt and film scene have on you.

	Novel excerpt	Film scene
Similarities		
Differences	content: perspective: realization:	content: perspective: realization:
Effects		

Possible solutions

	Novel excerpt	Film scene
Similarities	<ul><li>*WWM* show is depicted</li><li>told/shown from contestant's perspective (Jamal/Ram): – novel: Ram as first-person-narrator, e.g. "I can hardly see the audience …" – film: Jamal's perspective, e.g. through over-the-shoulder shots</li><li>with regard to content, e.g.: – host makes fun of Jamal/Ram – Jamal/Ram has a poorly paid job (difference: waiter/"chai-wallah") – "The audience begins clapping." – "The signature tune comes on and Prem Kumar's booming voice fills the hall." etc.</li></ul>	
Differences	content:<ul><li>three contestants mentioned, with Ram being the first</li><li>works as a waiter</li><li>first question is already asked (and differs from later questions in film)</li><li>name: Ram Mohammad Thomas (expresses diversity of India and its religions)</li></ul>	content:<ul><li>Jamal is the only contestant</li><li>works as a "chai-wallah"[1]</li><li>first question is not yet asked in this scene</li><li>name: Jamal Malik</li></ul>
	perspective:<ul><li>first-person narrator → feelings are described</li></ul>	perspective:<ul><li>feelings are shown and acted out</li><li>not only Jamal's perspective, but also that of the audience and of production staff/crew</li></ul>
	realization:<ul><li>in this extract, only *WWM* scene is shown[2]</li><li>you read about lighting and sound (e.g. "The audience begins clapping. There are some cheers and whistles, too.")</li></ul>	realization:<ul><li>cross-cutting/parallel action: *WWM* scenes (blue/black lighting) interrupted by torture scenes (yellow/brown lighting)</li><li>you really see the lights and hear the sounds (e.g. *WWM* motif)</li></ul>
Effects	<ul><li>insight into Ram's feelings through narrative perspective</li></ul>	<ul><li>showing and acting leads to sympathy with/feeling with/empathy for/… Jamal</li><li>mode of presentation creates (more) excitement and vibrancy</li></ul>

---

[1] i.e. he makes and serves chai = tea
[2] structure of the novel actually follows similar pattern with differences in content (parallel action between Ram's lawyer Smita and the studio)

Vikas Swarup: Q & A

The studio lights have been dimmed. I can hardly see the audience sitting around me in a circle. The hall is illuminated by one spotlight in the centre, where I sit in a leather revolving chair opposite Prem Kumar. We are separated by a semicircular table. There is a large screen in front of me on which the questions will be projected. The studio sign is lit up. It says 'Silence'.

'Cameras rolling, three, two, one, you're on.' The signature tune comes on and Prem Kumar's booming voice fills the hall. 'Here we are once again, ready to find out who will make history today by winning the biggest price ever offered on earth. Yes, ladies and gentlemen, we're ready to find out Who Will Win A Billion!'

The studio sign changes to 'Applause'. The audience begins clapping. There are some cheers and whistles, too.

The signature tune fades out. Prem Kumar says, 'We have three lucky contestants with us tonight, who have been selected at random by our computer. Contestant number three is Kapil Chowdhary from Malda in West Bengal. Contestant number two is Professor Hari Parikh from Ahmedabad, but our first contestant tonight is eighteen-year-old Ram Mohammad Thomas from our very own Mumbai. Ladies and gentlemen, please give him a big round of applause.'

Everyone claps. After the applause dies down, Prem Kumar turns to me. 'Ram Mohammad Thomas, now that's a very interesting name. It expresses the richness and diversity of India. What do you do, Mr Thomas?'

'I am a waiter in Jimmy's Bar and Restaurant in Colaba.'

'A waiter! Now isn't that interesting! Tell me, how much do you make every month?'

'Around nine hundred rupees.'

'That's all? And what will you do if you win today?'

'I don't know.'

'You don't know?'

'No.'

Prem Kumar scowls at me. I am not following the script. I am supposed to 'vibe' and be 'entertaining' during the 'small talk'. I should have said I will buy a restaurant, or a plane, or a country. I could have said I will host a big party. Marry Miss India. Travel to Timbuktu.

'OK. Let me explain the rules to you. You will be asked twelve questions, and if you answer each one correctly, you stand to win the biggest jackpot on earth: one billion rupees! You are free to quit at any point up until question number nine and take whatever you have earned up to then, but you cannot quit beyond question number nine. After that, it is either Play or Pay. But let's talk about that when we come to that stage. If you don't know the answer to a question, don't panic, because you have two Lifeboats available to you – A Friendly Tip and Half and Half. So I think we are all set for the first question for one thousand rupees. Are you ready?'

'Yes, I am ready,' I reply.

'OK, here comes question number 1. A nice easy one on popular cinema, I am sure everyone in the audience can answer. Now we all know that Armaan Ali and Priya Kapoor have formed one of the most successful screen pairings of recent times. But can you name the blockbusting film in which Armaan Ali starred with Priya Kapoor for the very first time. Was it a) *Fire*, b) *Hero*, c) *Hunger*, or d) *Betrayal*?'

The music in the background changes to a suspense tune, with the sound of a ticking time bomb superimposed over it.

'D. *Betrayal*,' I reply.

'Do you go to the movies?'

'Yes.'

'And did you see *Betrayal*?'

'Yes.'

'Are you absolutely, one hundred per cent sure of your answer?'

'Yes.'

There is a crescendo of drums. The correct answer flashes on the screen.

'Absolutely, one hundred per cent correct! You've just won one thousand rupees! We will now take a quick commercial break,' declares Prem Kumar.

The studio sign changes to 'Applause'. The audience claps. Prem Kumar smiles. I don't.

from: Vikas Swarup: Q & A. London, Random House UK, 2006, pp. 45–47

Component 1: Introducing a Slumdog's life

1.4 Background: The term "Slumdog" – discussing its connotations

Eine mögliche Vorbereitung der folgenden Aufgabe, in welcher der Begriff „Slumdog" diskutiert wird, wäre zum einen die Behandlung der Frage:

Where does the word "Slumdog" appear first?

Vermutlich werden die Schülerinnen und Schüler den Aufdruck „Slumdog Millionaire" auf dem Shirt eines der spielenden Jungen („freeze-frame") bemerkt haben. Ebenso wird der Begriff „Slumdog" bereits einige Sekunden vorher vom Polizeiinspektor während der Folterszene verwendet. Die dazu passenden Filmszenen könnten in diesem Zusammenhang noch einmal kurz gezeigt werden:

0:05:35 (police officer: "What the hell can a Slumdog possibly know?")
0:05:52 ("Slumdog Millionaire" on shirt of a kid from the slums)

Zum anderen bietet sich eine Brainstorming-Aufgabe zu dem Begriff „Slumdog" an, deren Ergebnisse an der Tafel oder am OHP gesammelt werden:

What comes to your mind when you hear the word "Slumdog"?

- poverty
- negative idea/association/connotation
- swearword/curse word
- animal which does not have a home/shelter
- cute (puppy)
- contrast to money/millionaire (if students refer to whole title)
- …

Als Hausaufgabe könnte den Schülerinnen und Schülern am Ende der Stunde *Copy 6* gegeben werden, deren Ergebnisse in der darauffolgenden Schulstunde besprochen werden.

Mögliche Antworten zu den Aufgaben auf *Copy 6*:

1. (mögliche Rückfragen: ICT? Indochina Time; IANS? Indo-Asian News Service)

2. • Indian people rather than e.g. British or German; people who live in the slums; people who work for social organizations
   • defaming slum inhabitants by giving them an animal name; they might see it as an insult; the name is against basic human values

3. • Beaufoy: metaphor; inspired by research in the slums;
   • Tandon: Jamal is called a "Slumdog" in the beginning; English translation of Hindi term for someone who lives in the slums

The term "Slumdog"

1. Read the following article and look up words in your dictionary if necessary.
2. Who might be offended by the term "Slumdog" and why?
3. Which reasons do Beaufoy and Tandon offer for choosing the term "Slumdog"?

'Slumdog …' title not offensive, but metaphor: scriptwriter

January 21st, 2009 – 10:46 pm ICT by IANS

Simon Beaufoy, the screenplay writer of Danny Boyle's Golden Globe winning "Slumdog Millionaire" Wednesday said the title of the film was only a "metaphor". "There was absolutely no sense I wanted to insult anybody. I just liked the idea of the metaphor (Slumdog)," Beaufoy told reporters here. "As a part of my research, I was wandering in the slums. I was very intrigued by the cats and dogs wandering around there, who dared to be asleep in the sunshine. Though they do look carefree from the outside, they are watching everything from the rims of their eyes," he said. "It is like somebody who is apparently not worthy of an existence but is actually looking at everything and eyeing everything out – just like the boy in the game show who knows everything not through intelligence but through experience. So, I just made up the word," he added.

Loveleen Tandon, the film's co-director, echoed the same sentiment and said: "'Slumdog' is the way the protagonist of the film is referred to. It's actually an English translation of the way we refer to a man from the street or a slum."

"He's looked upon as someone who wants nothing, and in order to say that, it's expressed in this kind of harsh way to make him feel like nothing. It's not that the film is trying to say that a man living in the slums is a dog," she explained.

Patna-based social worker Tapeshwar Vishwakarma, general secretary of the Jhuggi Jhonpdi Samyukta Sangharsh Samiti, earlier dragged "Slumdog Millionaire" to court, contending that the sensibilities of the slum dwellers have been offended by the movie title.

"I don't feel I've written a film about poverty. That never occurred to me. What I genuinely felt in my heart was the (slum) people's massive spirit and massive determination to overcome terrible troubles. That's how I approached it. 'Slumdog Millionaire' is a fairytale," said Beaufoy. […]

www.thaindian.com/newsportal/entertainment/slumdog-title-not-offensive-but-metaphor-scriptwriter_100145447.html

Further information:
- "The Real 'Slumdog Millionaire'"
  www.spiegel.de/international/world/0,1518,614355,00.html
- "Slum dweller finds 'Slumdog Millionaire' title abusive, sues"
  www.thaindian.com/newsportal/uncategorized/slum-dweller-finds-slumdog-millionaire-title-abusive-sues_100145178.html
- "Enthusiasm, criticism for film 'Slumdog Millionaire'"
  www.asianews.it/view4print.php?l=en&art=14292

1.5 Film analysis: Cinematic devices – *slum chase*

Die hier aufgeführten Arbeitsaufträge (*while-viewing tasks*) beziehen sich auf die *slum chase*-Szene in Kapitel 3 (0:05:51 – 0:07:50). Diese Szene ist aufgrund ihrer interessanten Kameraführung, Perspektiven und Musik/Geräuschen sehr gut für die Behandlung der Filmsprache und der dramatischen Wirkung filmtechnischer Mittel geeignet.

Es empfiehlt sich, den Schülerinnen und Schülern an dieser Stelle eine Übersicht mit *Selected terms for film analysis* auszuteilen (**Copy 7**), die sie im Vorfeld durchlesen sollten. Diese kurze Wiederholung der filmsprachlichen Mittel wird die Qualität der Antworten sicherlich verbessern.

Die Schülerinnen und Schüler erhalten die Tabelle auf **Copy 8**, in der sie während der erneuten Betrachtung der *slum chase*-Szene ihre Ergebnisse stichpunktartig erfassen können. Um die Schülerinnen und Schüler dabei nicht zu überfordern, bietet es sich an, ihre Aufmerksamkeit auf einen der folgenden Punkte zu lenken: *field sizes*, *point of view*, *camera angles*, und *camera movement*. Die Schüler können dabei je nach Interesse einen dieser Punkte auswählen, sodass sich vier Gruppen ergeben. Dabei muss nicht jede Zeile detailliert ausgefüllt werden; es reicht aufgrund der Vielzahl stilistischer Mittel aus, die besonders auffälligen und wirkungsvollen Stilmittel zu notieren.

Die Szene sollte mindestens zweimal gezeigt werden, damit die Schülerinnen und Schüler genügend Zeit haben, ihre Aufgabe zu bearbeiten. Im Anschluss sollten die Ergebnisse (z. B. im Plenum auf einer OHP-Folie) gesammelt werden. Dazu müsste die Szene punktuell noch einmal für alle gezeigt werden, wenn Veranschaulichungen notwendig werden.

Im Unterrichtsgespräch sollte abschließend über mögliche Wirkungseffekte der filmtechnischen Mittel reflektiert werden:

> Which atmosphere is created in the *slum chase*-scene?
> Which role do the cinematic devices play in creating these effects?

An dieser Stelle kann ebenfalls die spezielle Wirkung der eingesetzten Hintergrundgeräusche und Musik diskutiert werden. Um diese zu verdeutlichen, könnte man den *sound-off approach* für die Szene anwenden:

> How do sound and music have an impact on these effects?

The language of film: Selected terms for film analysis

1. Camera/image
1.1 Field sizes (*Einstellungsgröße/Bildausschnitt*)

extreme long shot (*Weitaufnahme/Panoramaaufnahme*): a view from a considerable distance, e.g. the skyline of a city

long shot (*Totale*): the camera is at a great distance from the subject being filmed and presents the entire setting

full shot (*Halbtotale*): a full view of a person; includes the entire body of a subject and not much else

American shot (*Amerikanische*): a three-quarter view of a person, showing her or him from the knees up

medium shot (*Nahaufnahme*): a view of the upper half of a person's body

close-up (*Großaufnahme*): the camera is very close to the object; full view of, typically, a human face

extreme close-up/detail shot (*Detailaufnahme*): a small object or part of an object shown large (a speaking mouth, a telephone number on an envelope)

1.2 Point of view (*Darstellungsperspektive*) establishing shot

generally a long shot that shows the general location of the scene that follows, often providing essential information, and orienting the viewer

point-of-view shot (POV): shows the scene from the point of view of a character

over-the-shoulder shot: the camera gets close to, but not fully into, the viewing position of a character

reaction shot: a shot showing a character reacting (with wonder, amusement, annoyance, horror, etc.) to what she/he has just seen

reverse-angle shot: a shot from the opposite side of a subject

1.3 Camera angles (*Kameraperspektive*)

eye-level/straight-on angle (*Normalsicht/Augenhöhe*): the camera is positioned at about the same height as the object (fairly conventional)

high angle/overhead (*Obersicht/Vogelperspektive*): objects and people are filmed from above; a limit case is a bird's-eye view taken from a helicopter or an airplane

low angle/below shot (*Untersicht/Froschperspektive*): objects and people are filmed from below

1.4 Camera movement (*Kamerabewegung*)

pan(ning) (*horizontaler Schwenk*): the camera moves from left to right or vice versa around the vertical axis

tilt (*vertikaler Schwenk*): the camera moves upwards (tilt up) or downwards (tilt down) around the horizontal axis

tracking shot/pulling shot (*Kamerafahrt*): the camera follows (tracks) or precedes (pulls) an object which is in motion itself

push in, pull back: the camera moves in on or away from a stationary object

zoom: not a camera movement, but a shift in the focal length of the camera lens to give the impression that the camera is getting closer to (zooming in) or farther from (zooming out) an object

1.5 Camera speed (*Aufnahmegeschwindigkeit*)

normal speed (*normale Geschwindigkeit*): the speed of the action corresponds to its real time

slow motion (*Zeitlupe*): the action takes more time than in reality; it is slowed down

fast motion (*Zeitraffer*): the action takes less time than in reality

freeze frame (*Standbild*): a still picture

1.6 Colour (*Farbgestaltung*)

black and white (*schwarz-weiß*)
colour (*Farbe*)
predominance of certain shades and tones (*Einfärbung*)

1.7 Lighting (*Beleuchtung, Lichtgestaltung*)

high key vs. low key (*starke vs. geringe Grundausleuchtung*): the whole scene is fully lit vs. not everything is fully lit (= indirect lighting, a certain darkness of the screen)
natural vs. studio light (*Tageslicht vs. Kunstlicht*)

2. Montage/editing

shot (*Einstellung*): the basic unit of a film; an uninterrupted sequence of action shown continuously
sequence (*Sequenz*): a larger unit of film composed of a number of shots which belong together (because of time, actors involved, setting, etc.)
cut (*Schnitt*): most common type of transition in which one scene ends and a new one immediately begins; a cut is the jump from one shot to the next
fade out (*Abblendung*) ... **fade in** (*Aufblendung*): the end of a shot is marked by fading out to an empty screen (usually black); there is a brief pause; then a fade in introduces the next shot
dissolve (*Überblendung*): a gradual transition in which the end of one scene is superimposed over the beginning of a new one
parallel action/cross-cutting (*Parallelmontage*): intermingling the shots of two or more scenes
flashback (*Rückblende*): a sequence of a film that goes back in time to show what happened earlier in the story
flash-forward (*Vorausschau*): scenes or shots referring to future time
match cut: two shots or scenes are linked by visual, aural or metaphorical parallelism

aus: Nünning, A., Surkamp, C.: Englische Literatur unterrichten – Grundlagen und Methoden © 2006 Friedrich Verlag GmbH, Seelze

Field sizes

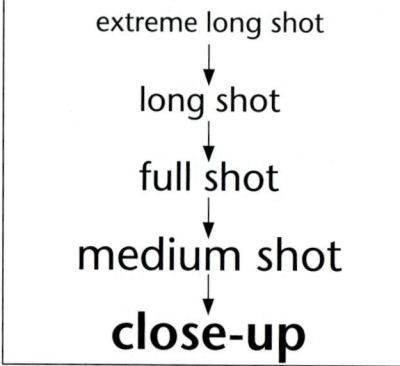

Camera movement

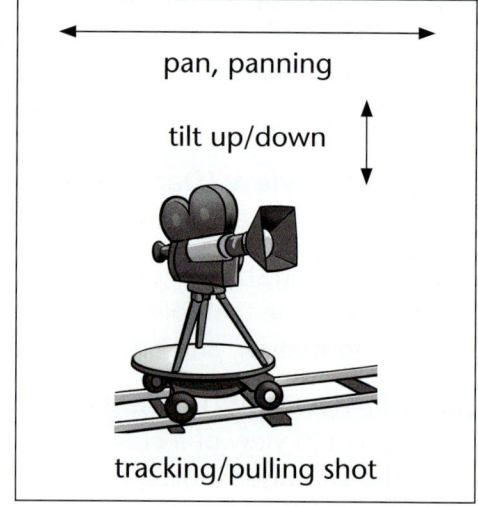

Camera angles

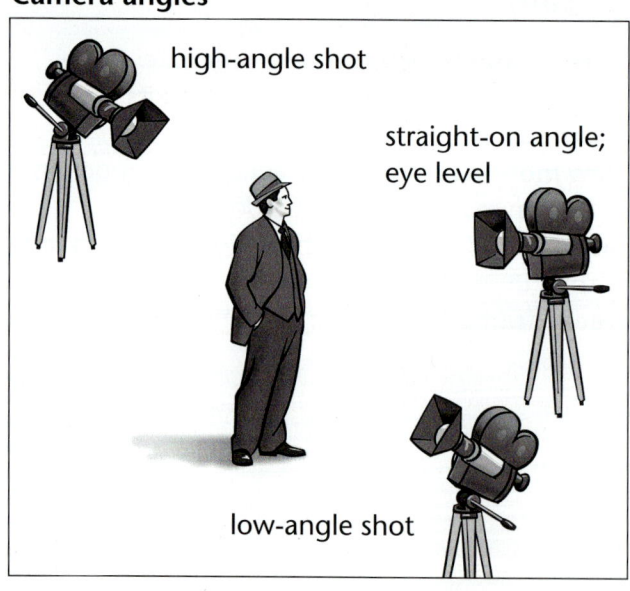

While-viewing tasks: Cinematic devices

Choose one of the categories of cinematic devices in the grid and fill in your column while watching the *slum chase*-scene.

	Field sizes	Point of view	Camera angles	Camera movement	Additional remarks
Boys playing at the airfield					
Police officers chasing boys on motorbikes					
Boys at waste dump jumping from roofs					
Chase through narrow streets					
Boys throwing waste on police officer					
Running along the river					
Chase on the pipeline					
Back in the narrow streets (dog and barber shots)					
Five shots of boys running in the slum's narrow streets					

Component 1: Introducing a Slumdog's life

While-viewing tasks: possible solutions

Diese Liste enthält keine vollständige Darstellung aller stilistischen Mittel der Szene, sondern beschreibt ausgewählte Einstellungen, die besonders auffällig sind und von den Schülerinnen und Schülern daher vermutlich identifiziert werden.

	Field sizes	Point of view	Camera angles	Camera movement	Additional remarks
Boys playing at the airfield	close-up (Jamal's face); extreme long shot (plane flying away)	reaction shot (Jamal/Salim); POV-shot (from Jamal's POV: ball flying through air; plane starting)	low angle/ below shot (ball flying through the air; plane starting)		freeze frame (boy in "slumdog millionaire"-shirt); slow motion (Jamal tumbling down)
Police officers chasing boys on motorbikes	long shot (boys running away with motorbike in left-hand corner); extreme long shot (boys, police officers and airfield); medium shot (Jamal); then close-up (Salim)	"reverse-angle shot"* (constant change of perspective between police and boys)		panning (preparing to run away); tracking shot; then pulling shot (boys running away); tilt up (Jamal)	
Boys at waste dump jumping from roofs			low angle/ below shot (boys jumping down from roof)	tilt up, then pan(ning) (boys arriving in the slum)	slow motion (boys jumping down from roof)
Chase through narrow streets			high angle/ overhead (three boys running); low angle/ below shot (Jamal/Salim running)	pulling shot (Jamal/Salim running); tracking shot (policemen chasing them)	sunlight blinding
Boys throwing waste on police officer		"over-the-shoulder shot"* (slum kids looking down on police officer);	high angle/ overhead (slum kids); low angle/ below shot (police officer looking up at slum kids)		

* not in the conventional sense

Component 1: Introducing a Slumdog's life

	Field sizes	Point of view	Camera angles	Camera movement	Additional remarks
		POV-shot (from the police officer's POV: slum kids throwing waste on him, waste falling down)			
Running along the river	long shot (young man in the river, boys running along the side of the river)			panning (policeman chasing boys); tilt up (woman dying clothes)	shot of young man lasts fairly long compared to the generally high frequency of cuts during the chase
Chase on the pipeline			change between high angle and straight-on angle shots (boys on pipeline)		
Back in the narrow streets (dog and barber shots)	full shot (dog in focus; boys in background out of focus); medium shot (upper half of the barber's body, boys in background)				pictures of everyday life (dog and barber) with shots of the chase in the background
Five shots of boys running in the slum's narrow streets	full shot gradually becomes extreme long shot		high angle becomes bird's-eye view		the distance between the slum and the camera increases with each cut

Effects:
- very vivid and almost chaotic atmosphere is presented with numerous cinematic devices; this feeling is intensified through the use of rather slow/calm scenes (slow motion, long-lasting shots of young man in river, woman dying clothes, dog, barber, etc.) which contradict the generally fast pace
- viewer is hurtled into the film due to the scene's dynamic and energetic atmosphere (NOTE: Danny Boyle originally intended to use this scene as the film's opening, cf. commentary)
- very intense (first) impression of slum life with the help of different field sizes (long shots: general setting; full/medium shots: details of

slum life; close-ups: facial expressions of slum boys → way of showing their feelings)
- viewer almost feels as if he/she were part of the chase due to camera work (camera movement: especially tracking and pulling; point of view)
- the typical image of the status/role of police officers and slum kids which the viewer might have in mind is reversed: slum kids find their way through the narrow streets, whereas authority figures seem to have problems orienting themselves; slum kids throw waste at police officer and the respective shots underline that he is made fun of (over-the-shoulder shot from a high angle with slum kids looking down on police officer; police officer sees waste falling down on him shot from a low angle)
- the fast music and the pulsating rhythm and beat in *O… Saya* emphasize the hectic atmosphere (mainly through the use of drums) and underline the spirit of the chase

Component 2
The three musketeers: "All for one, one for all"?

2.1 Content: Taking a closer look at the three musketeers

Im Rahmen von *Component 2* soll es inhaltlich um die Charakterisierung der drei Hauptfiguren Jamal, Salim und Latika sowie deren Beziehung untereinander gehen (2.1). Außerdem wird in *Component 2* eine Behandlung des religiösen und politischen Hintergrunds in Indien als landeskundlicher Einschub (2.2) in Verbindung mit einer Filmanalyse mithilfe des Audiokommentars von Danny Boyle (2.3) vorgeschlagen.

Diese Aufgabe trägt bereits zu Beginn des Films dazu bei, sicherzustellen, dass alle Schülerinnen und Schüler die „drei Musketiere" Jamal, Salim und Latika einschätzen können, sowie deren Beziehung untereinander verstanden haben. Dies gilt insbesondere für den Fall, dass die in *Component 1* vorgeschlagenen *long-term while-viewing* Aufgaben nicht behandelt werden. Eine den Film begleitende Aufgabe unter Verwendung von *Copy 9* könnte daher lauten:

> Fill in the boxes next to Jamal, Salim and Latika with any important information you can gather on these characters while watching Chapters 4–11. Please also pay attention to their relationships and write down (on the respective line of the triangle) all those incidents which help to characterize the relationships.

Die Ergebnisse der Schüler können im Anschluss auf einer OHP-Folie oder an der Tafel gesammelt werden. Dazu kann das Muster von *Copy 9* verwendet werden.

Weitere Informationen zu den drei Hauptfiguren sind weiter vorne im Heft unter „**Die Personen**" (S. 8f.) zu finden. Ausführlichere Charakterisierungen sind außerdem den Musterlösungen der *long-term while-viewing tasks 1–3* (*Component 1*, S. 33f.) zu entnehmen.

Jamal, Salim and Latika – their relationships

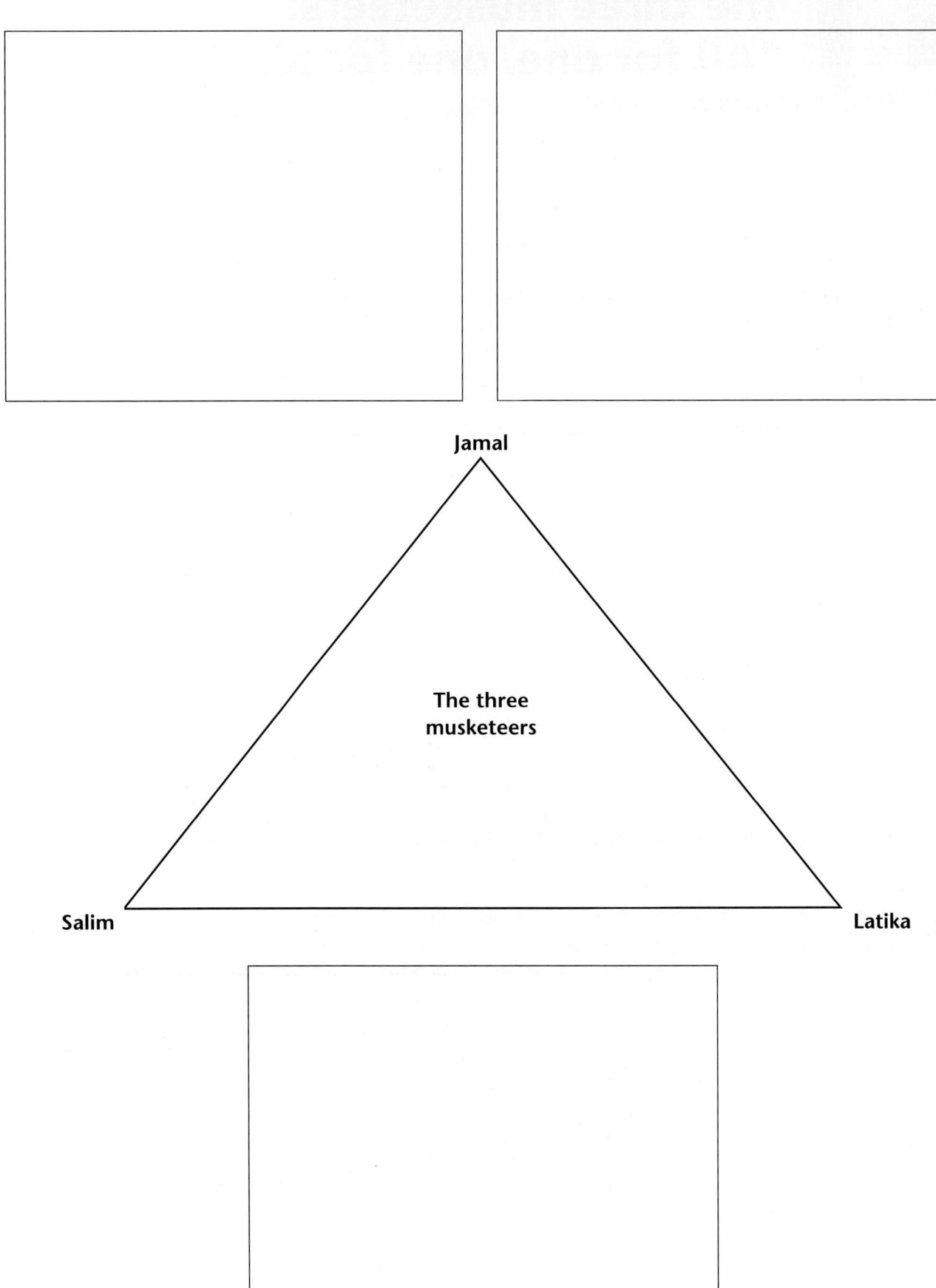

Eine mögliche Lösung für *Copy 9* könnte folgendermaßen aussehen:

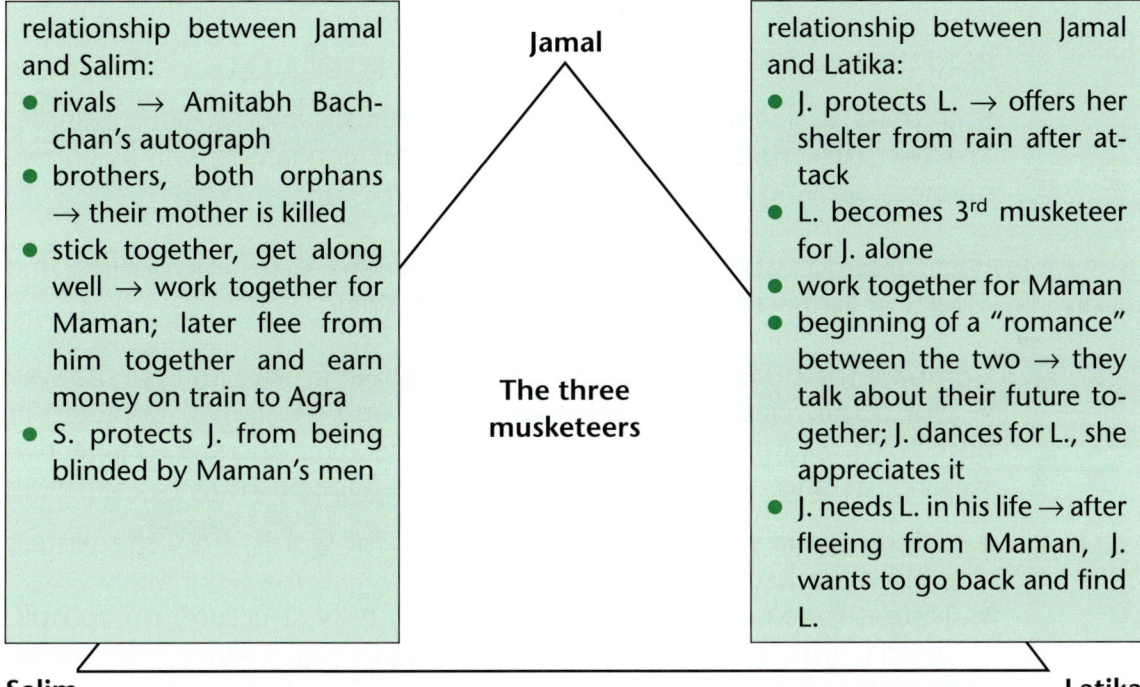

2.2 Background: The conflict between Hindus and Muslims in India

Eine brisante Filmszene ist der Angriff von hinduistischen Fanatikern auf ein muslimisches Slum, in dem Jamals und Salims Mutter ums Leben kommt. Der religiöse Konflikt zwischen Hindus und Muslimen spielt im Film keine wichtige Rolle, doch ist dieses Thema in Bezug auf Landeskunde und die politische Lage in Indien von großer Bedeutung im Englischunterricht und sollte deswegen eingehender behandelt werden. Es empfiehlt sich, diese Erörterung des religiösen und politischen Hintergrundes mit der Filmanalyse (Kapitel 2.3) zu verbinden, um die Unterschiede zwischen der Realität und der Darstellung im (fiktiven) Film zu verdeutlichen.

Die folgenden Texte (*Copy 10*) enthalten Hintergrundinformationen zum Konflikt zwischen Hindus und Muslimen. Sie nähern sich dem Thema jedoch auf eine sehr unterschiedliche Art und Weise, was natürlich auch durch die unterschiedlichen Textsorten bestimmt wird. Der erste Text ist ein Auszug aus einem Buch, das Rubina Ali, die Schauspielerin der siebenjährigen Latika, nach der Veröffentlichung des Films geschrieben hat. Dieser Text ist primär durch eine kindliche Sichtweise auf das Thema gekennzeichnet (siehe mögliche Antworten). Der zweite Text ist ein Artikel aus dem *TIMEasia Magazine*, der das Thema mit einigen konkreten Beispielen, Zahlen und Fakten darstellt (siehe mögliche Antworten).

Component 2: The three musketeers: "All for one, one for all"?

Die Bearbeitung der Texte wird nach dem ersten Ansehen der Kapitel 4–11 als Hausaufgabe gegeben und kann unter folgenden Fragestellungen erfolgen:

Read the two texts below and outline their overall topic.

Both texts deal with the conflict between Hindus and Muslims in India. The texts describe the circumstances of this conflict as well as consequences deriving from it.

In der folgenden Unterrichtsstunde sollten dann die unterschiedlichen Sichtweisen und stilistischen Aspekte in Partnerarbeit genauer untersucht werden.

Compare the book excerpt with the newspaper article. Analyse the way in which the relationship between Hindus and Muslims is depicted in both texts. Examine the two writers' perspectives and their respective styles of writing. What effects do both texts have on you?

- differences in sentence structure, choice of words, how the writers embed the issue into other topics
- 1st text (book excerpt): short sentences, easy structure, no complicated words; a child's view/childish style of writing; writer retells what her father has told her (father experienced attacks himself; writer did not); writer emphasizes that despite some tension between Hindus and Muslims, they generally live together peacefully; personal perspective on the topic (subjective): emotional bond to the reader is created by using the first-person-narrator; only one paragraph in her whole book which explicitly deals with the film *Slumdog Millionaire* and connections to reality
- 2nd text (magazine article): long sentences, separated in paragraphs; formal style; historical dates; facts and figures; although Muslims' grievances are depicted and justified, the text is more neutral (objective); degree of conflict and its effects are made clearer than in text 1 (e.g. number of victims is stated, discrimination, scapegoating); possible reasons and future developments are outlined; references to politics and job market are made; reader becomes aware of the extent of the conflict

Nachdem die Ergebnisse der Analyse an der Tafel oder auf Folie in Stichpunkten gesammelt wurden, können die Schülerinnen und Schüler sie in der Hausaufgabe in einem zusammenhängenden Text darstellen.

2.3 Film analysis: The depiction of the Hindu attack on the Muslim slum

Wie bereits in Kapitel 2.2 dargestellt wurde, ist die Filmszene, in der hinduistische Fanatiker den muslimischen Slum angreifen, in welchem Jamal, Salim und ihre Mutter leben, äußerst brisant. Diese Szene spielt nicht nur eine wichtige Rolle in Bezug auf ihren religiösen und politischen Hintergrund (siehe Kapitel 2.2), sondern bietet sich auch für eine genauere Analyse hinsichtlich ihrer filmischen Darstellung an, was für das Lernziel *film literacy* relevant ist. Es empfiehlt sich daher, zunächst den Hintergrund zu beleuchten, um danach die filmische Darstellung und Wirkung der Szene zu analysieren.

This excerpt was written by 9-year-old Rubina Ali who played the youngest version of Latika. Obviously, the book was published after the film had been released.

Text 1:

This film is a bit different from other Bollywood movies in that it shows real things. Like the issue of Hindus and Muslims fighting, and when the two heroes, Jamal and Salim, see their own mother die before their very eyes. In reality these fights did happen in the Mumbai slums. It was before I was born, but my father remembers it as if it hap-
5 pened yesterday. He told me about it. He was a teenager at the time when the Hindus and the Muslims had a big clash in our slum. My father ran to hide like everyone else. Some people had knives, others guns. Aba saw a man fall dead next to him, hit by a *goli* (bullet). Three of his neighbours were also killed. The police came, but they just added to the panic, killing more people. There were lots of children among the victims.
10 Since then everything has gone back to normal. The Hindus and Muslims live side by side without too many problems but there is still some tension. I sometimes wonder why they hate each other. We are all the same people from the same country, but I guess it is because there are some bad people in both communities. I have a few Hindu friends and I also celebrate Diwali, the festival of lights and crackers. You have to be careful of
15 crackers in the slums, though, or you could cause a huge fire. We set them off just outside, near the railway tracks.
As for the trafficking of handicapped children that you see in *Slumdog Millionaire*, that's all true too. [...]

Rubina Ali (with Anne Berthod and Divya Dugar): Slumgirl Dreaming. My Journey to the Stars. London, Black Swan, 2009, pp. 101–102

Text 2:

Hate thy neighbor –
Muslims feel the heat as India leans towards Hindu nationalism

The following text is taken from *TIMEasia Magazine*:

India has always prided itself on its secularism. But with the rise of a Hindu-chauvinist movement, animosity toward the country's 150 million Muslim minority has intensified. As a result, many Muslims feel more insecure than ever. Their key grievances include:
5 **GUJARAT** In retaliation for a Muslim attack on a train carrying Hindu pilgrims in February last year, Hindu mobs embarked on an orgy of murder, rape and arson against Gujarati Muslims, killing as many as 2,000.
AYODYHA In 1992 Hindu mobs destroyed a 16th century mosque in Ayodhya claimed by right-wing Hindu nationalists to have been built on the site of a temple that marked
10 the birthplace of the deity Rama. Nationwide riots ensued as Muslims protested; nearly 1,800 people were killed in Bombay alone. Then, in March 1993, the Muslim underworld detonated a series of bombs across Bombay, killing nearly 300 people. Hindus want to rebuild a temple on the disputed site, but preliminary archaeological findings have shown no sign of a previous temple there.
15 **JOB DISCRIMINATION** Although the constitution recognizes the right to equal opportunities, many Hindu-run companies don't hire qualified Muslims. Likewise, the government hires a disproportionate number of Hindus, exacerbating Muslims' sense that they are economically oppressed.
SCAPEGOATING Indian Muslims are often regarded as a potential fifth column for the
20 country's archenemy Pakistan. Accusations of collusion with Islamabad surface each time terrorists launch attacks on Indian soil.

www.time.com/time/asia/covers/501030811/neighbor.html, by Alex Perry, August 4, 2003

chauvinist 1. aggressive patriotism or blind enthusiasm; 2. biased devotion to any group, attitude or cause
animosity hostility, hatred
grievances actual or supposed circumstances regarded as just cause for complaint
retaliation return of like for like, esp. evil for evil; reprisal
arson the malicious burning of another's house or property
deity a god or goddess
Rama one of the most popular figures and deities in Hinduism
scapegoating the act or practice of assigning blame or failure to another, as to deflect attention or responsibility away from oneself
archenemy a chief enemy; a principal enemy

Component 2: The three musketeers: "All for one, one for all"?

 Für die Filmanalyse sollte die Filmszene (0:15:55 – 0:18:42) im Unterricht noch einmal gezeigt werden. Während des Anschauens können die Schülerinnen und Schüler sich stichwortartige Notizen zu Darstellung und Wirkung der Szene machen, um anschließend zu Hause einen zusammenhängenden Kommentar zur Szene schreiben zu können.
Die Fragestellung zu den stichwortartigen Notizen kann dabei wie folgt formuliert werden:

 While watching the scene carefully, take notes which refer to how the scene is depicted. Also, consider the effects the scene has on you.

 Hierzu könnte unten stehendes Beobachtungsschema vorgegeben werden. Nachdem die Filmszene gezeigt wurde und die Schülerinnen und Schüler sich Notizen gemacht haben, sollen ihre subjektiven Eindrücke und Analyseansätze in Bezug auf die Darstellung der Filmszene zunächst an der Tafel gesammelt werden.

What?/Who?	How?	Effect on viewer?
picture of slum, children playing, women washing clothes	long shot, high angle, voices and noise of playing children	lively and peaceful atmosphere
attack starts, Jamal rises out of the water, his mother is knocked down	dull sound, reaction shots, fast cuts; subtitle "They're Muslims, get them!"	we see Jamal's perspective of the scene; religious background (subtitles)
Jamal and Salim running away, people fighting, running, burning, being killed	fast cuts, panning, tracking and pulling shots; threatening music and sounds	chaotic, hectic, threatening, violent atmosphere
child in blue (god Rama)	reaction shots, reverse-angle shots, different mode/shade/tone	scene is viewed through the eyes of the children; dream-like, unreal, hallucination; hint at Hindu religion
dead mother in water/ Jamal back in police office	dissolve; sound fades out	traumatizing event for Jamal; connection between past and present

Die Stundenergebnisse können anschließend in der Hausaufgabe in einen zusammenhängenden Text einfließen:

 Recall the scene in which Jamal and Salim's mother is killed and comment on the way in which the conflict between Hindus and Muslims is depicted in this scene.

- religious conflict itself is not made very clear to us, as religious groups are not explicitly referred to (except for remarks in the subtitles); the figure of Ram/Rama hints at Hindu religion
- the boys' perspective is used for the scene: brutal, hectic/chaotic atmosphere (effect through usage of fast cuts); screams can be heard; muffled sound (→ the way the boys would hear it)

 In der nächsten Unterrichtsstunde sollten zunächst die Ergebnisse der Hausaufgabe besprochen, diskutiert und an der Tafel festgehalten werden. Daraufhin bietet es sich an, den

Audiokommentar von Regisseur Danny Boyle zu dieser Filmszene anzuhören (special features, audio commentary, chapter 6, 0:15:54–0:18:42), den die Schülerinnen und Schüler mündlich zusammenfassen sollen.
Achtung: Dieses DVD-Extra gibt es nur auf der UK-Version. Als Alternative kann der transkribierte Audiokommentar (Copy 11) verwendet werden.

Da im Grundkurs beim Hören Verständnisprobleme und Unklarheiten auftreten könnten, besteht die Möglichkeit, diese durch das nachträgliche Lesen des Kommentars (*Copy 11*) auszuräumen.
Danach wird diskutiert, ob sich die beabsichtigte Wirkung mit den Eindrücken der Schülerinnen und Schüler deckt (Vergleich mit den an der Tafel festgehaltenen Ergebnissen der Hausaufgabe) und inwieweit es dem Regisseur gelungen ist, diese von ihm beabsichtigte Wirkung zu erzielen:

> Compare your own first impressions of the scene with what Danny Boyle intended to achieve according to his audio commentary.

Die mündlich geäußerten Schülerergebnisse sollten in ein Tafelbild einfließen oder auf Folie gesammelt werden.
Wenn die Schülerinnen und Schüler dazu tendieren, dass Boyle die Wirkung erreicht hat, die er erzielen wollte, werden sie dies auf die von ihnen selbst genannten filmischen Mittel zurückführen (siehe mögliche Antworten zu der oben gestellten Aufgabe).
Sind die Schülerinnen und Schüler eher der Meinung, dass Boyle es nicht deutlich genug geschafft hat, diese Wirkung zu erzielen, könnten sie diskutieren, wie sie selbst als Regisseure die Szene abändern würden, um Boyles intendierte Wirkung tatsächlich bzw. überzeugender zu erreichen.
Eine weitere Möglichkeit, die Darstellung von ‚Religion' bzw. ‚religiösem Glauben' zu vertiefen, bietet sich am Ende der Unterrichtsreihe an, wenn der gesamte Film angeschaut worden ist. Dazu wäre eine Fragestellung denkbar, welche im Rückblick die Bedeutung der Szene im Kontext des gesamten Films thematisiert und darüber hinaus auf das Thema Religion/Glaube anspielt, das vor allem durch die Figur von Salim deutlich wird.
Folgende Aufgabe kann von den Schülerinnen und Schülern in Partnerarbeit bearbeitet werden, um danach die Ergebnisse im Plenum zu diskutieren:

> Try to recall the scene in which Jamal and Salim's mother is killed. Which role does the conflict between Hindus and Muslims play in the entire film?

- the religious conflict itself does not play a role in the film but religion/religious belief does, especially for Salim (when reuniting with Jamal: "God is good"; praying; last words: "God is great")
- the fact that their mother is killed is important for the plot of the film as it makes Jamal and Salim orphans who are now responsible for themselves; the attack itself makes Jamal and Salim run away and leads to getting to know Latika; Jamal apparently still suffers from this incident (when talking about his mother's death at the police station)

Danny Boyle: Audio commentary

While reading the transcript of the audio commentary by Danny Boyle, answer the following question: What are the director's aims of presenting the events in this particular way?

"This introduces one of our most challenging … kind of … sequences in the film, and especially with the violence that's been happening in India recently …
There are these incredible moments … of terrible violence which are often of a religious nature … Muslim slums are attacked, and occasionally, the Muslims react
5 and attack back, and … this is based on a number of cases of …, but it's not based on … any specific one …
But it is an attack upon a Muslim slum by a gang of Hindu, right-wing Hindu nationalists, fanatics …
And we did have a problem really as Westerners going in, dealing with something
10 as sensitive as this and … what we did and it was brilliantly done by Marco, our designer, is that he built this little bit of slum elsewhere so that we wouldn't upset any locals and we did it out in the countryside … and really the decision we took apart from that, which was obviously not to cause any local trouble by people getting the wrong idea of what we might be doing, is that we … we also then tried to view
15 the film …
The film tried to view it from the point-of-view of a 7-year-old:
He wouldn't understand any of the finer details of politics, nationalism, religious intolerance, bigotry … it's just the chaos. It's just kids who see their mum die and see people being terrorized and horrified and murdered … and they cannot make
20 sense of it … and they almost see … a hallucination almost, an imaginary figure of Ram, sort of like seeing themselves in the mirror almost, but dressed in the figure of Ram who's being invoked … by the raiders; whose name is being invoked in their cause … unfairly so, really, because generally it's an extraordinarily peaceful and calm country – despite the overcrowding, despite the poverty and the discrepancies
25 … and this is documented as well as supposedly the police did stand by at different times …"

Slumdog Millionaire, Pathé/Celador Films/Film 4, 2008, chapter 6, 0:15:54 – 0:18:42

Component 3
From Taj Mahal to Mumbai: A journey to the past

3.1 Content: Listening comprehension

Die Kapitel 12–17 des Films befassen sich inhaltlich mit den Brüdern Jamal und Salim im Alter von etwa 13 Jahren, die zunächst im und in der Nähe des Taj Mahal arbeiten und dabei auch nicht vor illegalen Handlungen zurückschrecken, wie z. B. dem Stehlen und Verkaufen von Schuhen und dem Irreführen von Touristen. Dabei spielen auch interkulturelle Begegnungen eine Rolle: So führt Jamal als „Reiseführer" beispielsweise deutsche Touristen durch den Taj Mahal und zeigt in einer anderen Szene amerikanischen Touristen die Gegend in Agra. Inspiriert von einer Freilichtoper, die Jamal wieder an Latika denken lässt, entschließt er sich, zusammen mit Salim nach Mumbai zurückzukehren, um dort nach seiner großen Liebe zu suchen. Bei seiner Suche bekommt der Zuschauer einige Eindrücke von der Stadt Mumbai. Dort finden Jamal und Salim schließlich Latika, fliehen mit ihr in ein Hotel, aus dem Salim seinen Bruder kurzerhand herauswirft.

In Bezug auf den sprachlichen Aspekt des Films endet mit DVD-Kapitel 12 der Teil des Films, der durch die Verwendung von Hindi und englischen Untertiteln dominiert wird. Jamal und Salim sprechen – auch untereinander – hauptsächlich Englisch. Die indische Varietät des Englischen kann mitunter eine Herausforderung für die Schülerinnen und Schüler darstellen. Um ihnen zum einen den Wechsel von Untertiteln auf das Verstehen der in verschiedenen Dialekten gesprochenen Sprache zu erleichtern und zum anderen das Verständnis zu sichern, bietet sich eine sehbegleitende Aufgabe an, in der die Schülerinnen und Schüler die auf *Copy 12* genannten Zitate verschiedenen Figuren zuordnen sollen und kurz den Kontext bestimmen, in denen das Zitat vorkommt.

Auf diese Weise erfassen die Schülerinnen und Schüler nicht nur den Inhalt der Filmsequenz, sondern schulen auch ihre *listening skills* und sind außerdem zum genauen Hinhören (*listening for detail*) motiviert.

Im Anschluss an das gemeinsame Anschauen der Kapitel 12–17 und dem parallelen Bearbeiten von *Copy 12* werden die Ergebnisse im Plenum besprochen und im Zweifelsfall entsprechende Szenen erneut gezeigt.

> **Lösungen zu *Copy 12*:**
>
> 1. "Is this heaven?"
>
>   **Jamal**. *He and Salim look at the Taj Mahal and speculate what it is.*
>
> 2. "Would it be possible to show us around now?"
>
>   **German tourist (woman)**. *Jamal is standing next to a sign which advertizes guided tours of the Taj Mahal. He is mistaken for a tour guide by the German couple.*

3. "But the swimming pool, as you can see, was completed on schedule in top class fashion."

   Jamal. *He pretends to be a real tour guide and invents stories about the Taj Mahal.*

4. "Well … here is a bit of the real America, son!"

   American tourist (woman). *She makes her husband give Jamal money.*

5. "It's funny, you don't seem that interested in money."

   Police officer. *He apparently begins to believe Jamal and wants to find out why Jamal is on the show.*

6. "Bombay had turned into Mumbai."

   Jamal. *He begins to tell the police officer why he knew the answer to the one-hundred-dollar-bill question.*

7. "There are 19 million people in this city, Jamal. Forget about her. She's history."

   Salim. *The brothers are working in a restaurant kitchen in Mumbai. Jamal wants to find Latika; Salim tries to convince him that this plan is hopeless.*

8. "You really thought you could just walk in and take my prize away? Have you any idea how much this little virgin is worth?"

   Maman. *He wants to prevent Jamal and Salim from escaping with Latika.*

9. "Maman never forgets … isn't that right?"

   Salim. *He threatens Maman with a revolver and does not believe Maman when he tells Salim that they can leave and he will forget about it.*

10. "You're a sweet boy, Jamal."

    Latika. *She comes out of the shower and takes the towel which Jamal offers her. She apparently appreciates that he looks away.*

11. "Did you really kill him? … Good. My enemy's enemy is a friend. Come here, my friend … I've been looking for someone like you."

    Javed. *He talks to Salim who has come looking for Javed and has just explained that he was the one who killed Maman. Javed is apparently going to hire Salim.*

12. "I never forgot – not for one moment. I knew I'd find you in the end. It's our destiny."

    Jamal. *He and Latika are in the hotel room and talk about their relationship.*

13. "I am the elder. I am the boss. For once, you do as I say. Now get

out!"

Salim. *He has come back into the hotel room in which Jamal and Latika are sleeping. He throws Jamal out in order to have Latika for himself.*

14. "You puzzle me, Slumdog. Admitting murder to avoid the charge of fraud is not exactly clever thinking. Now why would you do that?"

Police officer. *He wants to find out why Jamal is on the show.*

3.2 Background: Conducting an Internet research on Agra and Mumbai

Da die Handlung innerhalb der Kapitel 12–17 in den Städten Agra und Mumbai spielt, bietet es sich im Hinblick auf landeskundliche Inhalte Indiens an, die Schülerinnen und Schüler innerhalb von **Component 3** einige Hintergrundinformationen zur Stadt Agra und dem sich hier befindlichen Taj Mahal ebenso wie zur Entwicklung der Metropole Mumbai (vormals Bombay) erarbeiten zu lassen. Die Schülerinnen und Schüler werden sich im Anschluss an die Kapitel, in denen Jamal als angeblicher *tour guide* falsche Geschichten zum Taj Mahal erzählt, sicherlich nähere und zwar korrekte Informationen zum Taj Mahal sowie zur Stadt Agra wünschen. Außerdem wird ein Klärungsbedarf hinsichtlich des Satzes „Bombay had turned into Mumbai" bestehen.

Eine mögliche Herangehensweise wäre hier, die Schülerinnen und Schüler je nach Interesse zu einem dieser Themen eine Internetrecherche betreiben zu lassen, in der sie Daten und Fakten zu einer der beiden Städte zusammentragen und anschließend in der Klasse präsentieren. Für diese Internetrecherche sollte möglichst eine Doppelstunde eingeplant werden, für die Präsentation in der darauffolgenden Stunde mindestens eine weitere Schulstunde. Dabei kann je nach Lernausgangslage ein eher offenes und autonomes oder etwas gelenkteres Vorgehen, z. B. unter Vorgabe von Gruppengröße, *related links* und der späteren Präsentationsform, angebracht sein.

Generell bieten sich folgende Arbeitsaufträge an:

Internet research, choice 1:

You are the tour guide now. Go online and search the Web for some information on the Taj Mahal and additional background information on the city of Agra.
Here is a list of related links you might consider when conducting your Internet research:
- http://whc.unesco.org/en/list/252
- http://tourism.webindia123.com/tourism/monuments/tombs_minarets/tajmahal/index.htm
- http://asi.nic.in/asi_monu_whs_agratajmahal.asp
- www.youtube.com/watch?v=nzK6_OcgMow

Present your findings to the others next session. Prepare your presentation at home.

Internet research, choice 2:

It is your job to explain Jamal's phrase "Bombay had turned into Mumbai" to the other group. Please go online and search the Web for some

Who says what and in what context?

Write down the respective speaker and outline the context briefly.

1. "Is this heaven?"

_____

2. "Would it be possible to show us around now?"

_____

3. "But the swimming pool, as you can see, was completed on schedule in top class fashion."

_____

4. "Well … here is a bit of the real America, son!"

_____

5. "It's funny, you don't seem that interested in money."

_____

6. "Bombay had turned into Mumbai."

_____

7. "There are 19 million people in this city, Jamal. Forget about her. She's history."

_____

8. "You really thought you could just walk in and take my prize away? Have you any idea how much this little virgin is worth?"

_____

9. "Maman never forgets … isn't that right?"

_____

10. "You're a sweet boy, Jamal."

_____

11. "Did you really kill him? … Good. My enemy's enemy is a friend. Come here, my friend … I've been looking for someone like you."

_____

12. "I never forgot – not for one moment. I knew I'd find you in the end. It's our destiny."

_____

13. "I am the elder. I am the boss. For once, you do as I say. Now get out!"

_____

14. "You puzzle me, Slumdog. Admitting murder to avoid the charge of fraud is not exactly clever thinking. Now why would you do that?"

_____

information on the city of Mumbai and its development from Bombay to Mumbai.
Here is a list of related links you might consider when conducting your internet research:
- www.bl.uk/learning/histcitizen/trading/bombay/history.html
- http://en.wikipedia.org/wiki/Mumbai

Present your findings to the others next session. Prepare your presentation at home.

Mögliche Präsentationsformen wären zum Beispiel:

- Power-Point-Präsentation der Daten und Fakten
- Eine Stellwand mit Texten und Bildern aus dem Internet
- Ein Rollenspiel zwischen Fremdenführer und Tourist(en)

Für weitere Informationen zu Indien, z. B. zu einer Vertiefung der Person *Gandhi* (da dieser Name beispielsweise in Kapitel 13 im Zusammenhang mit indischen Geldscheinen auftaucht), sind außerdem folgende Linksammlungen zu empfehlen:
- http://bildungsserver.hamburg.de/englisch/linkssammlungen/
- http://deutschstunden.de/Links/Englisch/Landeskunde/Indien
- www.youtube.com/channel/UCMxJPchGLE_CJ1MJbJy-xDQ

Die Schülerlösungen werden je nach Präsentationsform und Kreativität der Schülerinnen und Schüler stark variieren. Inhaltlich sind die Ergebnisse den oben angegebenen Internetseiten zu entnehmen.

3.3 Film analysis: Subjective viewpoint

Der Zuschauer verfolgt den Film *Slumdog Millionaire* hauptsächlich aus der Perspektive des Hauptdarstellers Jamal Malik. Anders als in der Romanvorlage *Q&A*, in der Vikas Swarup seinen Hauptcharakter *Ram Mohammad Thomas* aus der Ich-Perspektive erzählen lässt, werden im Film verschiedene cinematographische Mittel für diesen Effekt benutzt. Möglich sind für die Erzielung dieses perspektivischen Effekts beispielsweise der Einsatz von sogenannten *voice-overs*, in denen Jamal spricht, ohne im Bild sichtbar zu sein, sowie von *over-the-shoulder shots, reaction shots* oder *point-of-view shots (POV;* vgl. **Copy 7**, S. 43 f.). Der *POV shot* zeigt dabei die Szene so, wie die Filmfigur sie sehen würde, weswegen man diese Einstellung auch als *subjective camera* bezeichnet. Dabei ist auch die Manipulation des Dargestellten, z. B. in Form eines verzerrten oder verschwommenen Bildes, üblich. Eine solche perspektivische Wirkung muss jedoch nicht lediglich durch visuelle Mittel erreicht werden. Andere Möglichkeiten dazu bestehen in der Manipulation der diegetischen Musik und Geräusche, also derjenigen *sounds*, die dem Film inhärent sind. Ist, wie in unserem Falle, der Hauptdarsteller bzw. die Hauptdarstellerin das Subjekt dieses *POV shots,* so handelt es sich um einen sogenannten *subjective viewpoint* des Films: Die Zuschauerinnen und Zuschauer sehen die Ereignisse quasi „durch die Brille" von Jamal, fast so als ob sie selbst daran Anteil hätten.
Eine geeignete Szene für die Analyse des *subjective viewpoint* ist die Szene, in der Jamal und Salim nach Latika suchen und sie von ihrem Zuhälter Maman entführen, indem Salim diesen erschießt. Jamal ist im Film nach dem Mord sichtbar fassungslos, schockiert und steif vor Angst. Diese Szene in Kapitel 15 beginnt bei 0:53:45, als Jamal und Salim sich der Türe nähern und durch das Schlüsselloch gucken und endet bei 0:56:43, bevor die Studioszene eingeblendet wird. Dieser Ausschnitt könnte im Anschluss an das erste Sehen der Kapitel

12–17 noch einmal gezeigt und unter folgender Arbeitsanweisung und unter Zuhilfenahme von *Copy 7* analysiert werden:

You are going to see the red light district scene again in which Salim shoots Maman and the brothers then rescue *Cherry* (Latika). The point of view changes throughout this scene. List those cinematic devices which are used to make you see the event from Jamal's point of view and which make you sympathize with him.

Die Ergebnisse werden im Unterrichtsgespräch gesammelt. Mögliche Schülerantworten könnten hier sein:

- reflection of dancing Latika in Jamal's eye when peeping through the keyhole
- shaky camera when grabbing Latika's things and putting them in the bag in a hurry
- over-the-shoulder shot when Maman and his men enter
- low-angle shot of Maman (the way Jamal would see him because he is smaller than Maman)
- reaction shot: Jamal looks scared when Maman talks to him and grabs his arm; tears in his eyes and heavy breathing out of fear when Salim takes out his revolver
- POV shot when Jamal looks in the mirror and witnesses the murder
- dull sounds, e.g. of the shot, and heavy breathing audible (the way Jamal would hear it because he covers his ears and is so shocked)
- reaction shot: Jamal looks scared and shocked
- hectic camera movements while Jamal is stiff with fear

Component 4
A roller coaster ride from rags to raja

4.1 Content

In Szene 23, der *bathroom scene*, kommt es zu einem interessanten Gespräch zwischen Prem Kumar, dem Gastgeber der Show *WWM*, und Jamal. Diese Szene ist für die weitere Entwicklung der Charaktere im Verlauf des Films von großer Bedeutung, da man hier einen guten Einblick in die Vergangenheit und Charakterzüge von Prem Kumar bekommt und insbesondere weil deutlich wird, welch gute Menschenkenntnis Jamal hat. Es bietet sich an dieser Stelle somit an, einen inneren Monolog von Jamal schreiben zu lassen, um zu diagnostizieren, ob die Schülerinnen und Schüler dem bisherigen Verlauf folgen konnten und sich in Jamals Gedanken und Gefühle hineinversetzen können. Der hierbei anzustrebende Perspektivenwechsel ist auch im Hinblick auf die Ausbildung von *intercultural communicative competence* von Bedeutung.
Die Schülerinnen und Schüler erhalten folgende Aufgabenstellung:

> Write a short interior monologue about Jamal's feelings and thoughts in this scene. As you are writing from Jamal's perspective, try to make sure to use his style and appropriate content.

Den Schülerinnen und Schülern wird daraufhin der Beginn von Szene 23 bis zu der Stelle gezeigt, an der Jamal den Buchstaben B auf dem Spiegel sieht und nachdenklich schaut (01:24:48–01:26:23). Sie haben dann ca. 10 Minuten Zeit, um einen inneren Monolog zu schreiben.
Da die Schülerinnen und Schüler zu diesem Zeitpunkt noch nicht wissen, wie der Film weitergehen wird, können sie sowohl davon ausgehen, dass Prem lügt, als auch, dass er die Wahrheit sagt und Jamal tatsächlich helfen möchte. Dies hilft ihnen bei der Antwort, da sie selbst in einer ähnlichen Situation wie der unwissende Jamal sind. Die Schülerantworten werden hier stark variieren. Folgende Stilmöglichkeiten sind besonders wahrscheinlich:

- *stream-of-consciousness*-Schreibstil
- sehr persönlicher Stil wie bei einem Tagebucheintrag
- viele Fragen, die darauf hindeuten, dass Jamal nicht sicher ist, wie er mit der „Hilfe" von Prem Kumar umzugehen bzw. wie er diese zu deuten hat
- ein möglicher Ausschnitt aus einer Schülerantwort könnte lauten: "I feel so sick … will I ever see Latika again? Oh, Latika, love of my life! I don't know the answer … feel so bad. Can I trust this guy? … Suddenly so nice? …"

Inhaltlich werden vor allem folgende Punkte in den Lösungen erscheinen:

- Nachdenklichkeit: Vertrauen schenken oder nicht; was sind Prem Kumars Beweggründe, die richtige oder falsche Antwort vorzugeben
- Gefühle: z. B. Angst, vielleicht nicht das Richtige zu tun; Verzweiflung, Latika bei falscher Antwort nicht mehr wiederzusehen

- über alte Zeiten nachdenken
- nach Lösungen zur korrekten Beantwortung der Quizfrage suchen: z. B. welche *lifeline* ist noch übrig; was könnte mögliche Antwort sein
- einen Entschluss fassen: Prem sagt die Wahrheit, ich vertraue ihm; *oder* Prem ist ein Lügner, ich wähle eine andere Antwort als B

4.2 Background: Globalisation

In den Kapiteln 18–23 begegnen dem Zuschauer mehrere Aspekte, die typisch für Globalisierung und ihre Merkmale sind.

So arbeitet Jamal, nun als 18-Jähriger, in einer britischen Telekommunikationsfirma, die in Mumbai ansässig ist. Die Firma schult ihre Mitarbeiter in britischer Landeskunde und bezüglich regionaltypischer Besonderheiten, um bei Telefongesprächen glaubwürdig zu wirken (Kapitel 18).

Auch das Wachstum der Millionenstadt Mumbai wird thematisiert und kann damit als Beispiel für die Entwicklung von Millionenstädten dienen: In Kapitel 19 sieht der Zuschauer Jamal und Salim, die in einem noch im Bau befindlichen Hochhaus sitzen und auf ihre Stadt hinunterschauen. Dabei sprechen sie über den Slum, in dem sie einmal gewohnt haben und der nun Wolkenkratzern gewichen ist.

Ein weiteres, den ganzen Film durchziehendes Merkmal von Globalisierung betrifft die Quizshow *Wer wird Millionär?*. Sie wird in mehr als 100 Ländern weltweit ausgestrahlt und sieht überall sehr ähnlich aus, da es hinsichtlich Studiodesign, Musik, Kamerafahrten und Beleuchtung strenge Vorgaben der Produktionsfirma gibt, die für alle Länder gelten. Diese Angleichung ist typisch für Globalisierungsprozesse im Kommunikations- und Mediensektor und hat vor allem wirtschaftliche Gründe, da Rechte und Anteile eine große Rolle beim Abschluss von Werbeverträgen und damit bei Geldströmen spielen. In diesem *Component* könnte auf die genannten Aspekte zu *Wer wird Millionär?* einerseits im Zusammenhang mit den Szenen, die Jamal in der Show zeigen (Kapitel 18, 21 und 23), eingegangen und andererseits erkannt werden, dass *Who Wants to Be a Millionaire?* in Javeds Villa im Fernsehen läuft, als Jamal Latika wiedersieht (Kapitel 20).

Um die Aufmerksamkeit der Schülerinnen und Schüler auf die genannten Aspekte im Zusammenhang mit Globalisierung zu lenken, können zunächst vor dem Sehen typische Merkmale von Globalisierung in einer Brainstorming-Phase gesammelt werden. Da das Phänomen der Globalisierung in verschiedenen Schulfächern behandelt wird und Kenntnisse darüber in vielen Lerngruppen vorausgesetzt werden können, kann diese einleitende Fragestellung auch übersprungen und direkt der Arbeitsauftrag für das fokussierte Ansehen der nächsten Filmkapitel gestellt werden.

What are typical aspects of globalisation? Above all, think of globalising processes with regard to economic developments and the media sector.

Economic developments: global companies; outsourcing; tourism; international banks; growth of cities; skyscrapers in which big companies have their offices; poverty in developing countries; gap between the rich and the poor

Media sector: the same films and TV series are shown and watched all over the world; TV shows follow a very similar pattern and have very similar structures and production schemes, e.g. game shows, quiz shows

Um einen Zusammenhang zu *Slumdog Millionaire* herzustellen und die Schülerinnen und Schüler in ihrer Wahrnehmung für den Aspekt der Globalisierung zu sensibilisieren, wird der folgende Arbeitsauftrag gestellt. Dieser soll von den Schülerinnen und Schülern während des Sehens mit stichwortartigen Notizen oder auch in Form einer Mind-Map bearbeitet werden, die zu Hause noch einmal überarbeitet wird.

> While watching the following chapters, pay special attention to aspects in the film which are typical of globalisation.

Aspects of GLOBALISATION in *Slumdog Millionaire*

Outsourcing: British telecommunication company (Jamal works there): staff has to know about Scotland as they call people there	**Quiz show *Who Wants to Be a Millionaire?***: structure of the show is similar to the *WWM* format which we have in Germany: e.g. similar way of asking questions; similar music/sound	**Growth of the city of Mumbai**: Jamal and Salim's slum does not exist anymore; business and skyscrapers everywhere; importance of India in global processes (at least Salim thinks so: "India is at the centre of the world")

Apart from the aspects within the film and within its plot, the film *Slumdog Millionaire* itself is an example of globalising processes: A British director makes a film together with an Indian crew (e.g. co-director, composer) and Indian actors; *Slumdog Millionaire* has been shown in cinemas all over the world and has won several awards from different countries, i.e. it was internationally successful.

4.3 Film analysis: Chapter 19

Um die Schülerinnen und Schüler im Umgang mit filmischen Mitteln und ihren Effekten zu schulen, ist ein konzentriertes Sehen unerlässlich. Um *Copy 13* auszufüllen, ist Aufmerksamkeit in Bezug auf die verwendeten filmischen Mittel einerseits und im Hinblick auf deren Wirkung andererseits erforderlich. Deswegen sollten die zu analysierenden Filmszenen für die Arbeit mit *Copy 13* zweimal angesehen werden.

Nachdem nun die Kapitel 18–23 angesehen und bearbeitet wurden (gegebenenfalls unter Berücksichtigung der in 4.1 und 4.2 vorgeschlagenen begleitenden Behandlung verschiedener inhaltlicher Aspekte), wird vor einem erneuten Ansehen des Kapitels 19, in welchem sich Jamal und Salim als ca. 18-Jährige wiedersehen, *Copy 13* verteilt. Die Schülerinnen und Schüler finden auf dem Arbeitsblatt *true/false-statements*, die es zu verifizieren bzw. zu falsifizieren gilt. Sie sollen zunächst die Behauptungen durchlesen und sich vergewissern, dass sie alle Begriffe kennen. Abhängig vom Vorwissen der Schülerinnen und Schüler müssen ggf. vereinzelt Begriffe geklärt werden.

Erst dann wird das Kapitel 19 angeschaut und *Copy 13* bearbeitet. Dabei bietet sich nachfolgende Aufgabenstellung an, die von der Lehrperson an die jeweilige Lerngruppe angepasst werden kann (z. B. könnte bei Lerngruppen, die mit Filmanalyse vertraut sind, die Klärung der Begriffe wegfallen).

Before you watch this part of the film twice, read the statements below and make sure you know all of the terms.

While watching this part of the film for the first time, pay special attention to the cinematic devices. Put a T for true or an F for false in the box next to each statement. In the case of a false statement, add the proper cinematic devices which are used in the scene.

During the second viewing, concentrate on the effects which the cinematic devices might have. Take notes which refer to these effects.

Nach dem zweimaligen Ansehen des Kapitels 19 bekommen die Schülerinnen und Schüler noch einige Minuten Zeit, um ihre Notizen auf *Copy 13* zu überarbeiten und zusammen mit einem Partner zu überprüfen. Danach werden die Ergebnisse im Plenum ausgetauscht und diskutiert. Evtl. ist ein erneutes Ansehen zur Klärung der Ergebnisse erforderlich.

Lösungen zu *Copy 13*:

1. The elevator which Jamal uses to get on the upper storey of a half-constructed building in order to meet Salim is filmed from a low angle.

   False. *It is filmed from above, i. e. high angle/overhead. This creates the impression that one is looking down on the elevator and gives the viewer a feeling of the height of the building.*

2. When Salim turns around and looks at Jamal, an over-the-shoulder shot is used.

   True. *It depicts the scene from Jamal's perspective, especially through the use of a close-up of Jamal's face before and a reverse-angle shot after the over-the-shoulder shot.*

3. In a 'fantasy scene', we see the brothers falling off the building. During the fall, there is a point-of-view shot from Salim's perspective and a close-up of Jamal's face which makes us feel as if we were falling off the building ourselves.

   False. *During the fall, there is a low angle/below shot first in which we see the two brothers and parts of the building from below. Afterwards, an (extreme) long shot shows the characters and further buildings from a greater distance. These cinematic devices show the extreme height from which they fall down and thus underline the dramatic effect of this scene.*

4. After Jamal has knocked down Salim, there is a freeze frame of both Jamal and Salim.

   False. *First, Jamal is filmed from a low angle/below shot, which makes us feel as if we are looking up at him ourselves. Then, Salim is filmed from a high angle/overhead shot which makes us feel as if we are looking down on him ourselves. There are also reaction shots in which we see Jamal's angry, disappointed, frustrated face and Salim's surprised, even shocked face. These shots clearly reveal what the two brothers feel at this very moment.*

5. When Jamal and Salim are sitting on the floor, looking down on the city, a pan is used.

   True. *This panning emphasizes the dimensions of the city and the height of the skyscrapers. Furthermore, it underlines Salim's words "I am at the centre of the centre".*

6. When Javed Khan is mentioned in the brothers' conversation, there is a dissolve to Javed sitting in a car.

   False. *It is not a dissolve, but a flashback which shows Javed in a car and Jamal and Salim as little boys crashing into that car. Moving between past and present makes the viewer feel as if past and present almost co-existed.*

7. In this part of the film, there is very happy music which underlines the joyful atmosphere.

   False. *The only "music" we hear are the sounds of the city (e.g. someone singing) and the ring-tone of Salim's mobile. Thus the conversation between the two brothers is the focus and the "natural" sounds of the city underline this authentic atmosphere.*

Chapter 19: Film analysis

True or false?
While watching this part of the film, pay special attention to the cinematic devices. Put a T for true or an F for false in the box next to each statement. In the case of a false statement, add the proper cinematic devices which are used in the scene and take notes which refer to these effects.

1. The elevator which Jamal uses to get on the upper storey of a half-constructed building in order to meet Salim is filmed from a low angle.

   _____

   _____

2. When Salim turns around and looks at Jamal, an over-the-shoulder shot is used.

   _____

   _____

3. In a 'fantasy scene', we see the brothers falling off the building. During the fall, there is a point-of-view shot from Salim's perspective and a close-up of Jamal's face which makes us feel as if we were falling off the building ourselves.

   _____

   _____

4. After Jamal has knocked down Salim, there is a freeze frame of both Jamal and Salim.

   _____

   _____

5. When Jamal and Salim are sitting on the floor, looking down on the city, a pan is used.

   _____

   _____

6. When Javed Khan is mentioned in the brothers' conversation, there is a dissolve to Javed sitting in a car.

   _____

   _____

7. In this part of the film, there is very happy music which underlines the joyful atmosphere.

   _____

   _____

Component 5

A triangle of money, love, and destiny

5.1 Content: The role of money, love, and destiny for Jamal and Salim

Die drei Aspekte Geld, Liebe und Schicksal ziehen sich wie ein roter Faden durch den gesamten Film. Jedoch gibt es deutliche Unterschiede zwischen der Bedeutung, welche die Brüder Jamal und Salim jeweils dem Geld, der Liebe und dem Schicksal beimessen. Werden die *long-term while-viewing tasks* nicht bearbeitet, können die Schülerinnen und Schüler während des Ansehens der letzten Kapitel (24–28) die beiden *triangles of money, love, and destiny* (*Copy 14*) ausfüllen. Der Arbeitsauftrag lautet:

> What are Jamal and Salim's respective attitudes towards the three overall themes of money, love, and destiny? Fill in the gaps while watching the last five chapters of *Slumdog Millionaire*.

Bearbeiten die Schülerinnen und Schüler bereits während des Sehens andere Sehaufträge, so empfiehlt es sich, die Dreiecke erst im Anschluss an das gemeinsame Ansehen ausfüllen zu lassen, um die Schülerinnen und Schüler nicht zu überfordern und ihnen so vermutlich den Spaß am Anschauen des Films zu nehmen. Je nach Leistungsstand ist auch ein arbeitsteiliges Vorgehen möglich, sodass die Schülerinnen und Schüler nach Interesse eine der beiden Figuren wählen und nur hierzu jeweils das Dreieck ausfüllen.

> **Mögliche Lösungen zu Jamal:**
>
> - Money: is not interested in money; does not seem to care much about winning the 20 million rupees on the show
> - Love: is constantly thinking about Latika (even at the police office → flashback to him desperately trying to find her at Javed's house); his love for Latika, not the money he might win, made him participate in *WWM* (Jamal: "I went on the show because I thought she'd be watching"; he smiles when reading the final question on the three musketeers even though he does not know the answer; he seems happy and relieved when he hears Latika's voice on the phone saying "I'm safe" and, in Hindi, "I'm yours" and is not frustrated that she doesn't know the answer to the question either); he never gives up trying to find the love of his life (Salim: "That guy, he will never give up"); waits for Latika at the VT station after having won on the show
> - Destiny: believes in destiny (Jamal's last words to Latika in the film: "This is our destiny"; on the screen: "D: It is written")
>
> **Mögliche Lösungen zu Salim:**
>
> - Money: money is important to him (he fills the bathtub with money to die in it)

Component 5: A triangle of money, love, and destiny

- Love: does not generally believe in love; finally realizes how strong the love between Jamal and Latika is and helps them reunite
- Destiny: does not talk about destiny, but has a very strong religious belief (needs salvation before his death → to Latika: "… and for what I've done, please forgive me"; last words: "God is great")

Im Anschluss an die Bearbeitung von *Copy 14* und an die Ergebnissicherung kann ein nächster Schritt die Behandlung des *overall theme of destiny* sein, welches durchweg eine wichtige Rolle im Film spielt. Hierzu können an der Tafel alle Filmausschnitte zum Thema gesammelt werden, an die sich die Schülerinnen und Schüler im Anschluss an das gemeinsame Ansehen erinnern können. Die auf diese Weise erfolgende Rekapitulation des gesamten Films kann zum Beispiel im *Think-Pair-Share*-Format stattfinden. Die Aufgabenstellung hierzu lautet:

Recapitulate all instances in which destiny plays a role in the film. First, note down individually what you can remember, then discuss your findings with your neighbour.

Im Plenum sollten dann, nachdem den Schülerinnen und Schülern genug Zeit gelassen wurde, um Ideen zu sammeln, die Ergebnisse gesammelt und an der Tafel festgehalten werden. Sollte die Zeit dies erlauben, ist es außerdem angebracht, relevante Szenen erneut kurz zu zeigen. Es könnten u. a. folgende Punkte zum Thema *destiny* im Film genannt werden:

- title card from the beginning of the film (0:00:42): "Jamal Malik is one question away from winning 20 million rupees. How did he do it? A: He cheated. B: He's lucky. C: He's a genius. D: It is written." ("It is written" → metaphor for destiny)
- Jamal and Latika (age 13) in hotel room talking about their relationship and destiny
- destiny/fate that all *WWM* questions refer to incidents in Jamal's life
- romantic scene towards the end (chapter 27): "D: It is written." (combines the topics of love and financial success, which in the film both depend on destiny)
- final scene:
  Jamal Malik: I knew you'd be watching.
  Latika: I thought we would meet only in death.
  Jamal Malik: This is our destiny.
  Latika: Kiss me.
  (Jamal believes in destiny throughout the whole film.)

Zum Abschluss könnte man kurz (erneut) das Filmposter zeigen (s. *Getting started*, S. 3), auf dem steht: „What does it take to find a lost love? A: Money, B: Luck, C: Smarts, D: Destiny", und die Schülerinnen und Schüler darüber diskutieren lassen, was für Jamal ausschlaggebend war, um seine verlorene Liebe wiederzufinden.

Triangles of money, love, and destiny

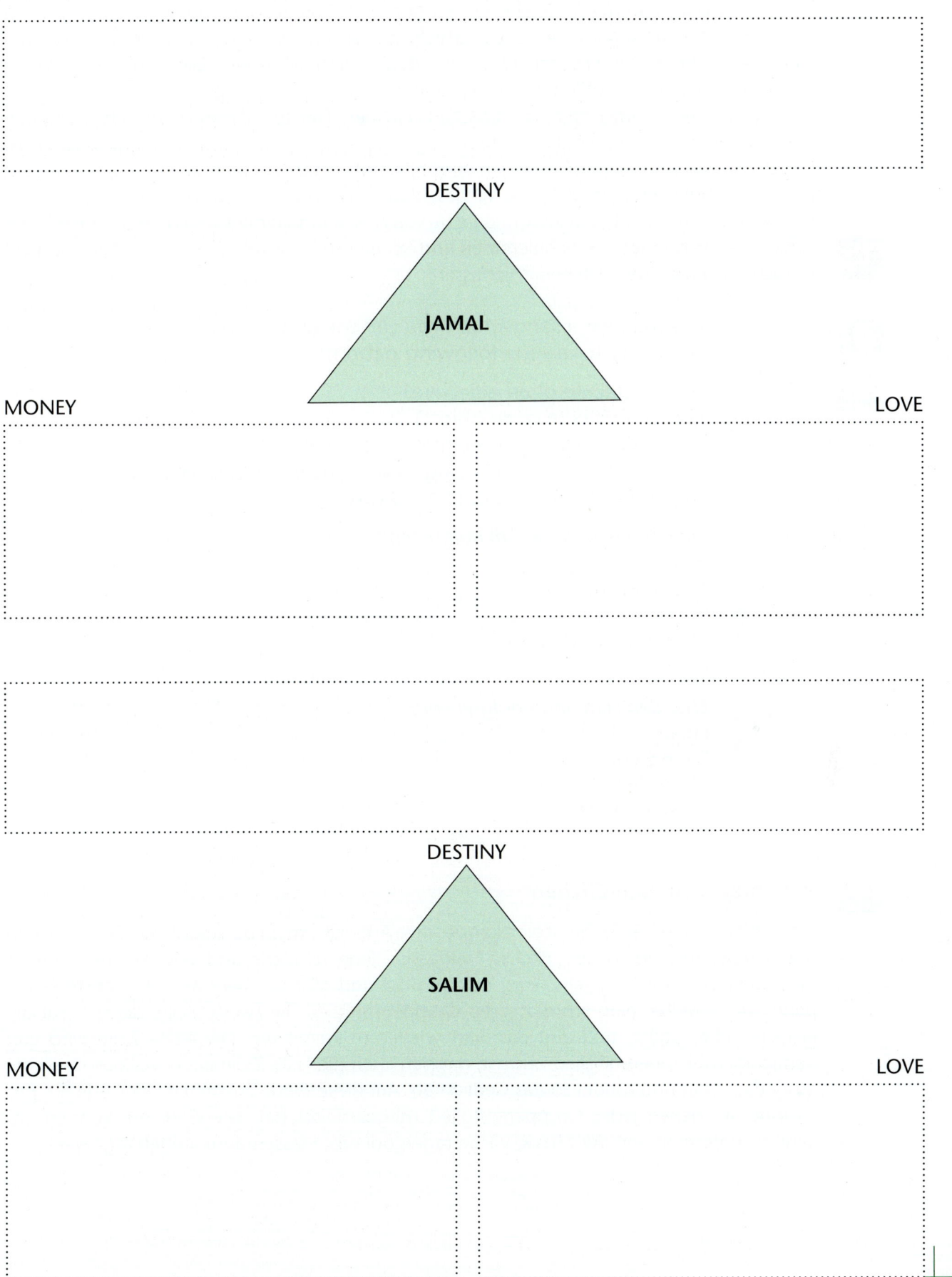

5.2 Background: The song *Jai Ho*

Das Lied *Jai Ho*, das während des Abspanns gespielt und zu welchem dabei getanzt wird, stieß auf großes Lob. Der indische Komponist A. R. Rahman, der für seine Filmmusik zu *Slumdog Millionaire* sogar einen Oscar erhielt, gewann für das hauptsächlich auf Hindi gesungene *Jai Ho* außerdem den Oscar für den besten Filmsong. Die Popmusik-Gruppe „Pussycat Dolls" veröffentlichte einen englischsprachigen Remix des Liedes, der unter dem Titel *Jai Ho! (You Are My Destiny)* in die Charts einstieg. Der Text dieses Liedes scheint jedoch nicht unbedingt für den Englischunterricht geeignet, da er kaum inhaltliche Anknüpfungspunkte an den Film bietet. Deswegen wird hier statt einer Auseinandersetzung mit diesem Lied eine schülerzentrierte Aufgabe vorgeschlagen, welche die Kreativität der Schülerinnen und Schüler fördert und den Filmsong *Jai Ho* von A. R. Rahman mit Fantasie und sprachlichen Fähigkeiten verbindet. Die Schülerinnen und Schüler sollen inspiriert von dem Filmsong ein Gedicht in Form eines „Elfchens" verfassen:

You will hear a song which you can use as an inspiration to write a short poem. Try to use the following pattern:

ONE WORD (e.g. an adjective)
TWO WORDS (e.g. an object)
THREE WORDS (e.g. describing the object)
FOUR WORDS (e.g. referring to the lyrical I, to people in general)
ONE WORD (e.g. result, conclusion)

Eher den Bollywood-Stil aufgreifend:
Fast
The rhythm
It catches me
Makes my body move
Joyful

Eher den Filminhalt aufgreifend:
Finally
Found you
My sweet musketeer
Love of my life
Destiny

Variante: „Gruppen-Elfchen"

Eine Variante dieser Aufgabe ist eine kooperative Arbeitsform, in der jeweils vier Schülerinnen und Schüler zusammen vier „Elfchen" verfassen. Jede Schülerin und jeder Schüler schreibt dazu die erste Zeile, d.h. ein Wort, auf ein Blatt und gibt das Blatt an das nächste Gruppenmitglied weiter. Nun schreibt jedes Gruppenmitglied die zweite Zeile, die sich auf die erste beziehen sollte, und gibt das Blatt wiederum weiter etc. Die letzte Zeile wird von demjenigen Gruppenmitglied verfasst, das sich auch die erste Zeile des jeweiligen Gedichts ausgedacht hat und rundet so das Gedicht ab. Auf diese Weise entstehen vier Gedichte pro Gruppe, an denen jedes Gruppenmitglied mitgearbeitet hat. Die Gedichte können am Schluss, untermalt von der Musik, vorgetragen oder im Klassenraum aufgehängt werden.

5.3 Film analysis: Chapters 24–27

Durch die Bearbeitung der folgenden sehbegleitenden Aufgaben wird der letzte Teil des Films noch einmal unter filmanalytischer Perspektive betrachtet. Dabei wird die Aufmerksamkeit auf zentrale filmische Darstellungsmittel gelenkt.
Nachdem der ganze Film einschließlich des Endes und des Abspanns angeschaut worden ist und gegebenenfalls 5.1 und 5.2 bearbeitet worden sind, werden die folgenden Aufgaben den Schülerinnen und Schülern zugänglich gemacht. Während des zweiten Sehens der Kapitel 24–27 können sich die Schülerinnen und Schüler stichwortartig Notizen machen, die sie anschließend in einer Stillarbeitsphase vervollständigen. Danach werden die Ergebnisse in Partnerarbeit ausgetauscht bzw. gegenseitig verbessert und schließlich im Plenum gesammelt.

> General task: Analyse the major cinematic devices and determine their effects.
>
> 1. Explain the use of parallel action/cross-cutting in the last chapters of the film.
>
>   The use of cross-cutting makes the viewer aware that there are several things happening at the same time:
>
>   - Jamal is taken back to the studio, Latika is driving to the studio; the WWM production staff prepares for the show, the audience nationwide prepares to watch the show
>   - Jamal is back on the show, preparing to answer the last question, Salim is in the bathroom, preparing for his death, Latika watches the show from the streets, then talks to Jamal on the phone
>   - Jamal guesses and wins while Salim kills Javed and is killed himself: Jamal wins money and finds Latika while his brother loses his life
>
>   Altogether, the cross-cutting mode creates a lively and even hectic atmosphere which underlines the plot.
>
> 2. There are flashbacks on Jamal's, Salim's and Latika's childhood. What is their function?
>
>   The flashbacks underline the connection of the past with the present: for example, the two brothers used to read "The Three Musketeers" at school, and now, the last WWM question is on the three musketeers. Also, we are reminded of the first encounter between Jamal and Latika (match cut: "My name is Latika"). The flashbacks at the very end when Jamal crosses the platforms make us recall different scenes and again show how Jamal has managed to answer the questions and thus find Latika.
>
> 3. How is Jamal and Latika's reunion at the VT station presented?
>
>   When Jamal sees Latika who is obviously looking for him, too, Latika's motif is used, which underlines the emotional situation. All the time, Jamal keeps looking at Latika, just as he kept looking for her during the past years. This scene is interrupted by flashback shots which connect past and present and make us recall how Jamal has managed to find Latika (siehe oben, Antwort zu *flashbacks*). There are several close-

ups of their faces, which stresses their feelings. At the end, there is a freeze frame of them kissing. This close-up is presented like a painting through the use of a reduction in colour saturation and a structure which resembles an oil-painting. This shot indicates that this is the very end of the film and underlines the very romantic, fairytale-like atmosphere.

4. Why do you think the rewind mode is used here?

Jamal kisses Latika's scar, and the rewind mode brings us back to a high angle shot of Latika which is used throughout the film. It seems as if Jamal recalled this situation and would like to reverse it.

5. What is the function of the title card saying "D: It is written."?

Its meaning refers to what Latika and Jamal have just said: "This is our destiny". Moreover, it refers to the very beginning of the film when another title card provides the question on how Jamal has managed to be one question away from winning 20 million rupees. Things have come full circle. Altogether, the overall theme of destiny is stressed here.

 Als Hausaufgabe bietet sich an, die Notizen in einen zusammenhängenden Text zu übertragen.

Component 6

Post-viewing activities

6.1 Presentation of *long-term while-viewing tasks*

Die Ergebnisse der *long-term while-viewing tasks* (mögliche Ergebnisse s. *Component 1*, S. 33 ff.) werden von den Schülerinnen und Schülern mündlich vorgetragen. Dabei sollten Visualisierungsmöglichkeiten wie Plakate, OHP-Folien, Tafelbilder oder PowerPoint genutzt werden, um Präsentationstechniken zu üben und den Zuhörern das Nachverfolgen der Ergebnisse zu erleichtern. Auch Filmszenen oder Filmmusik können bei der Präsentation zum Einsatz kommen, was vor allem für die Expertengruppe „Music & sound" wünschenswert ist. Nach jeder Präsentation sollten die inhaltlichen Ergebnisse von der gesamten Lerngruppe ergänzt und diskutiert werden. Auch ist eine Rückmeldung der Zuhörer zur Art und Weise der Präsentation möglich (*peer assessment*). Hierbei sollte z. B. auf freies Sprechen, Verständlichkeit und Formen der Visualisierung eingegangen werden.

6.2 Quiz questions in *WWM* format

Das folgende Quiz im Stil der Show *Wer wird Millionär?* kann zur Leistungsüberprüfung im Anschluss an das gemeinsame Anschauen des Films benutzt werden. Anders als bei gewöhnlichen Tests ist hier neben der Überprüfung auch der Spaßfaktor sehr hoch.

Es empfiehlt sich folgende Vorgehensweise:
Den Schülerinnen und Schülern wird das Format (1 Frage, jeweils 4 Antwortmöglichkeiten) anhand einer beispielhaften *quiz card* (s. *Copy 16*) erläutert. Die *quiz cards* können auch als Erwartungshorizont für mögliche Schülerergebnisse der folgenden Aktivität herangezogen werden.
Jede Schülerin und jeder Schüler erhält eine DIN A6 große Karteikarte, auf die oben eine Frage und darunter 4 Antwortmöglichkeiten zu schreiben sind. Auf der Rückseite wird dazu die korrekte Antwort notiert. Die Schülerinnen und Schüler sollten ermutigt werden, möglichst herausfordernde Fragen zu stellen. Für diese Aufgabe kann man *Copy 15* in ausreichender Zahl kopieren, schneiden und verteilen.
In Partnerarbeit tauschen die Schülerinnen und Schüler dann ihre selbst erstellten *quiz cards* aus, um sie vom Partner Korrektur lesen zu lassen (*peer correction*). Dabei sollten sie sowohl auf inhaltliche als auch auf linguistische Fehler achten und den Partner bzw. die Partnerin darauf hinweisen.
Die Karteikarten werden daraufhin von der Lehrperson eingesammelt und die Vorderseite auf OHP-Folien kopiert. Die Rückseite der Originalkarten wird in der gleichen Anordnung auf Papier kopiert. Diese korrekten Lösungen erhält der Moderator der Quiz-Show (Lehrerin/Lehrer oder Schülerin/Schüler) in der nächsten Stunde.

Alternativ möglich ist eine weniger schülerzentrierte, jedoch unkompliziertere und ebenfalls motivierende folgende Vorgehensweise:
Die Fragen zu „Who wants to be an expert on *Slumdog Millionaire* and India?" (*Copy 16*) werden auf Folien gezogen und am OHP schrittweise präsentiert.

75

Component 6: Post-viewing activities

Die korrekten Lösungen (s. *Copy 17*) bekommt nur der Moderator (Lehrerin/Lehrer bzw. eine Schülerin oder ein Schüler).

Zur Durchführung des Quiz:

Alle Schülerinnen und Schüler bekommen in der nächsten Schulstunde Karten mit A, B, C, D (s. *Copy 18*), welche dabei helfen, das Quiz interaktiver und spannender zu machen. Aus eigener Erfahrung ist es sinnvoll, die verschiedenen Buchstaben auf unterschiedlich farbiges Papier zu drucken (z. B. A auf rotes Papier, B auf blaues, C auf gelbes, D auf grünes).
Die Schülerinnen und Schüler stehen alle auf. Die 1. Quizfrage wird gestellt bzw. am OHP aufgedeckt. Alle Schülerinnen und Schüler müssen sich nun individuell die ihrer Meinung nach korrekte Antwort überlegen und die entsprechende Karte mit dem Buchstaben A, B, C oder D hochhalten. Durch die unterschiedlichen Farben der Karten kann der Lehrer bzw. die Lehrerin schnell sehen, ob jemand falsch oder richtig liegt. Diejenigen, die richtig geantwortet haben, dürfen stehen bleiben; die anderen müssen sich setzen. Dies geht so lange, bis die letzte Quizfrage gestellt wurde oder bis der letzte Schüler bzw. die letzte Schülerin noch steht. Dem Gewinner kann man dann eine kleine Belohnung geben.

6.3 Trailer

Der Filmtrailer, den man unter den *Special Features* der hier verwendeten DVD-Version finden kann, kann auch für eine *pre-viewing activity* genutzt werden (vgl. *Component 1*). In diesem Unterrichtsmodell erfolgt die Auseinandersetzung mit dem DVD-Begleitmaterial jedoch als *post-viewing activity* mit folgendem Arbeitsauftrag:

Now that you have seen the whole film, watch the movie trailer twice and answer the following questions:

1. What are typical features of trailers in general?

2. In how far does the trailer for *Slumdog Millionaire* adhere to these features (e.g. you might discuss whether it is an appropriate summary of the movie)?

3. What would you do differently if you were to create a trailer for *Slumdog Millionaire* and why?

1. • form: summary of the plot; shows the main characters; no chronological order necessary
   • production/marketing: name of the film and its director is stated; date of release (in case of trailers presented in the cinema); mentions well-known actors who belong to the cast; states number of awards the film has won; includes snippets of film reviews which praise the film; synopsis of spectacular scenes that are appealing to the potential viewer and attract him or her to watch the film; not revealing the ending to whet the viewers' appetite

2. • it mostly adheres to these typical features
   • what is missing: does not mention the actors' names; does not state number of awards
   • what is special about this trailer: it makes use of the ticking clock sound of *WWM* at the beginning (it plays with form)

3. • *answers may vary*

Question: _____ _____ _____?	Question: _____ _____ _____?
A: B: C: D:	A: B: C: D:
Question: _____ _____ _____?	Question: _____ _____ _____?
A: B: C: D:	A: B: C: D:
Question: _____ _____ _____?	Question: _____ _____ _____?
A: B: C: D:	A: B: C: D:

Quiz questions on "Who Wants to Be an Expert on *Slumdog Millionaire* and India?"

Welcome to … "Who Wants to Be an Expert on *Slumdog Millionaire* and India?"

☺

1. Where does most of the story take place?

   A: Mumbai

   B: New Delhi

   C: Calcutta

   D: Darjeeling

2. How many Oscars did *Slumdog Millionaire* win?

   A: Three

   B: Five

   C: Eight

   D: Ten

3. What is the main cinematic device of the film?

   A: Long shot

   B: Freeze frame

   C: Flashback

   D: Zoom

4. How does Jamal's mother die?

   A: Killed by Hindus

   B: Starvation

   C: She's just old

   D: Lung cancer

5. Who is the director of the film?

   A: Steven Soderbergh

   B: Alfred Hitchcock

   C: Roland Emmerich

   D: Danny Boyle

6. What are Salim's last words?

A: Allah's great!

B: Inch Allah!

C: Hare Rama!

D: God is great!

7. What is Jamal's job in Mumbai?

A: Call centre agent

B: Taxi driver

C: Assistant *(chai wallah)*

D: Facility manager

8. What is the title of the novel which *Slumdog Millionaire* is based on?

A: The White Tiger

B: Q & A

C: A Mighty Heart

D: City of Joy

9. What is the name of the gangster who recruits Salim and Jamal to work as beggars?

A: Javed

B: Maman

C: Amitabh

D: Prem Kumar

10. What is Jamal's faith?

A: Hindu

B: Muslim

C: Christian

D: Jewish

11. What is Latika's name while working in the brothel?

A: Sweety

B: Peachy

C: Cherry

D: Honey

12. In which city is the Taj Mahal located?

- A: Agra
- B: Mumbai
- C: Ayodyha
- D: Delhi

13. India has an estimated population of 1.2 billion. How many of them are Muslims?

- A: approx. 4 %
- B: approx. 13 %
- C: approx. 24 %
- D: approx. 38 %

14. Where can Latika meet Jamal every day at 5 pm?

- A: Victoria Terminus Station
- B: St. Elizabeth Hospital
- C: James Street
- D: Charles Station

15. What is Latika watching when Jamal visits her at Javed's house?

- A: A Bollywood movie
- B: Who Wants to Be a Millionaire?
- C: Tennis
- D: Golf

16. What is the song from the "Bollywood" dance scene called?

- A: Jai Ho!
- B: Paper Planes
- C: O... Saya
- D: Aaj Ki Raat Hona Hai Kya

17. Final question – Have a guess: What is the excrement really made of into which Jamal jumps?

- A: Mixture of water and mud
- B: Mixture of peanut butter and chocolates
- C: Mixture of wet paint and small pieces of wood
- D: Bolognese sauce

Correct answers for quiz questions on "Who Wants to Be an Expert on *Slumdog Millionaire* and India?"

1. Where does most of the story take place?

   A: Mumbai
   B: New Delhi
   C: Calcutta
   D: Darjeeling

2. How many Oscars did *Slumdog Millionaire* win?

   A: Three
   B: Five
   C: Eight
   D: Ten

3. What is the main cinematic device of the film?

   A: Long shot
   B: Freeze frame
   C: Flashback
   D: Zoom

4. How does Jamal's mother die?

   A: Killed by Hindus
   B: Starvation
   C: She's just old
   D: Lung cancer

5. Who is the director of the film?

   A: Steven Soderbergh
   B: Alfred Hitchcock
   C: Roland Emmerich
   D: Danny Boyle

6. What are Salim's last words?

   A: Allah's great!
   B: Inch Allah!
   C: Hare Rama!
   D: God is great!

7. What is Jamal's job in Mumbai?

   A: Call centre agent

   B: Taxi driver

   C: Assistant *(chai wallah)*

   D: Facility manager

8. What is the title of the novel which *Slumdog Millionaire* is based on?

   A: The White Tiger

   B: Q & A

   C: A Mighty Heart

   D: City of Joy

9. What is the name of the gangster who recruits Salim and Jamal to work as beggars?

   A: Javed

   B: Maman

   C: Amitabh

   D: Prem Kumar

10. What is Jamal's faith?

    A: Hindu

    B: Muslim

    C: Christian

    D: Jewish

11. What is Latika's name while working in the brothel?

    A: Sweety

    B: Peachy

    C: Cherry

    D: Honey

12. In which city is the Taj Mahal located?

    A: Agra

    B: Mumbai

    C: Ayodyha

    D: Delhi

13. **India has an estimated population of 1.2 billion. How many of them are Muslims?**

    A: approx. 4 %

    B: approx. 13 %

    C: approx. 24 %

    D: approx. 38 %

14. **Where can Latika meet Jamal every day at 5 pm?**

    A: Victoria Terminus Station

    B: St. Elizabeth Hospital

    C: James Street

    D: Charles Station

15. **What is Latika watching when Jamal visits her at Javed's house?**

    A: A Bollywood movie

    B: Who Wants to Be a Millionaire?

    C: Tennis

    D: Golf

16. **What is the song from the "Bollywood" dance scene called?**

    A: Jai Ho!

    B: Paper Planes

    C: O… Saya

    D: Aaj Ki Raat Hona Hai Kya

17. **Final question – Have a guess: What is the excrement really made of into which Jamal jumps?**

    A: Mixture of water and mud

    B: Mixture of peanut butter and chocolates

    C: Mixture of wet paint and small pieces of wood

    D: Bolognese sauce

A	A
B	B
C	C
D	D

6.4 Film reviews

Als abschließende *post-viewing activity* eignet sich eine Analyse und eigene Erstellung einer *film review*. Zunächst wird den Schülerinnen und Schülern dazu eine Filmkritik aus dem Internet verteilt (**Copy 19**), auf die sie in Form eines Blog-Kommentars reagieren sollen (*Schritt 1*). Darauf aufbauend erarbeiten sie eine Übersicht mit den wichtigsten Elementen einer *film review* und mit den einzelnen Schritten, die für das Verfassen ihrer eigenen Filmkritik wichtig sind (*Schritt 2*). Im Rahmen eines weniger schülerzentrierten Unterrichts kann die Lehrerin bzw. der Lehrer auch **Copy 20** (*How to write a review*) benutzen. Am Ende dieses Components steht schließlich die Erstellung einer eigenen *film review* (*Schritt 3*).

Schritt 1:
Als Vorbereitung auf das Schreiben einer eigenen *film review* kann eine Filmkritik (**Copy 19**) ausgeteilt werden. Um die Authentizität des Textes, der aus dem Internet stammt, beizubehalten, wurde hier auf Vokabelhilfen verzichtet. Bevor die Schülerinnen und Schüler auf die detaillierte Analyse von Filmkritiken eingehen und ihre eigene Filmkritik verfassen, können sie ihre erste spontane Reaktion auf die Filmkritik in Form eines Blog-Eintrags verarbeiten. Der Arbeitsauftrag dazu könnte beispielsweise folgendermaßen gestellt werden:

> Imagine you find this film review while surfing the Internet and you feel that you need to comment on certain aspects of this review. Write your own blog entry in which you state your opinion about aspects of *Slumdog Millionaire*.

Die Blog-Einträge der Schülerinnen und Schüler könnten wie folgt aussehen:

1. I enjoyed the unpredictable journey through the ups and downs of Jamal's life because I both suffered and laughed with him. I was emotionally drawn into Jamal's life and his experiences because it all appeared so real and authentic. However, at the end of the film, I began to cast doubt on the whole story when Jamal finally meets Latika at the station. In contrast to the reviewer, I think that this "final giddy flourish" destroys it all: It seems artificial and unconvincing. Together with the dancing scene in the credits, the end of the film makes you realize very quickly that it's just a movie – this sudden insight is disappointing in a way as it takes you back to reality far too quickly. Altogether, I liked the film – but I think the ending ruins it.

2. I don't agree with what the reviewer calls "shakier elements". In my opinion, the actors in the central love story are stunning! The love story is beautifully staged and the actors' shy acting underlines the respect which they have for each other. For me, they are the most beautiful and most convincing couple of the year!

'Is that your final answer?'

Slumdog Millionaire (2008) Directed by Danny Boyle
Starring: Dev Patel, Anil Kapoor, Irfan Khan and Freida Pinto

Interested in a big screen version of *Who Wants to be a Millionaire*? Perhaps you're looking for a gritty coming of age journey? Do you like foreign language flavored arthouse dramas? Do adrenaline-fueled flashback/flash forward adventures pique your interest? Perhaps you're not fussy about genres so long as True Love conquers all? If any of this appeals to you then *Slumdog Millionaire* might just hit your sweet spot. [...]

Slumdog tells the rather hard to swallow story of an orphan boy in Mumbai – his mother is murdered very early in the picture – who competes on his country's franchise of the global *Millionaire* phenomenon. Miraculously he knows all the answers without so much as a grade school education. The game show is concerned that he's cheating and, to allay their suspicions, Jamal (*Skins* star Dev Patel) explains how he came to know the answers. The film toggles between this investigation, the actual game show and multiple vignettes about his childhood and adolescence that reveal how he came by these very random answers.

Though *Slumdog* comes to us from the UK and is mostly filmed in India, it's a Hollywood picture through and through. Jamal is in essence an exotic mutation of Hollywood's crowded gene pool of idiot savants. Think *Forrest Gump*, *Rain Man* or any number of characters who lived by their wits and natural abilities, exceeding far beyond their intelligence, training and education levels. In short: it's a fairy tale.

British director Danny Boyle began his career making gleefully sadistic/amoral pictures like *Shallow Grave* and *Trainspotting*. His films are far less anarchic now but the through line in his filmography is the energy. *Slumdog*'s shakier elements – its somewhat disturbing core beliefs about fate and learning but also the very limited emotional palette served up by the actors in the central love story – are easy to ignore with so much happening on the screen. And so quickly, too! Boyle keeps the energy flowing throughout and the pace is always brisk. The editor Chris Dickens gets a real workout on his Avid. The cumulative effect of so much frenzied editing (this is but a step away from an action movie) is numbing. The production design by Mark Digby and the cinematography by Anthony Dod Mantle have a similar more is more and then less equation. At first you want to dive into the gorgeously saturated colors but as the movie progresses, the line between "gorgeously saturated" and "garish" starts to look a little blurry.

Slumdog's overt enthusiasms trip it up on more than one occasion. One unfortunate scene involving the fate of Jamal's brother is so overtold, slo-mo'ed and crosscut it plays as self-parodic of a big dramatic moment. The story's redundant insistence on reinforcing the comfort food of the "everything happens for a reason" belief system also makes the plot so deterministic that the audience feels like a presumptuous afterthought. [...] Jamal's journey is D-E-S-T-I-N-Y ... nothing you feel and no plot obstacle dreamed up could possibly alter it.

With so many of the movie's strengths also doubling as weaknesses, the final impression is crucial. Fortunately, Danny Boyle nails his dismount. The final giddy flourish in *Slumdog*, so wisely withheld, well judged and utterly cinematic, proves a giddy endearing release from the tense, relentless movie before it. You'll leave the theater on a high ... even if, like me, you weren't so sure about the preceding two hours.
Nathaniel R.
www.thefilmexperience.net/Reviews/slumdog.html

Schritt 2:
Die Schülerinnen und Schüler erstellen nun in Kleingruppenarbeit ihre eigene Übersicht (je nach Interesse, z. B. in Form einer *mind map* oder Tabelle) zu den wichtigsten Elementen und Aspekten, die in einer *film review* enthalten sein sollten. Hierzu kann man ihnen den folgenden Arbeitsauftrag erteilen:

> Take another look at the film review and, in groups of three to four, describe aspects and elements which should be incorporated into a film review. Try to illustrate your results with a picture (e.g. in a mind map or table).

Der Lehrer bzw. die Lehrerin fragt zunächst, welche Gruppe ihre Ergebnisse direkt auf einer OHP-Folie notieren und im Anschluss an die Gruppenarbeitsphase präsentieren möchte, und unterstützt in der Arbeitsphase die Schülerinnen und Schüler, indem er bzw. sie herumgeht und Hilfestellungen anbietet. Im Plenum werden die Ergebnisse dann präsentiert und im Unterrichtsgespräch werden weitere mögliche Aspekte von den anderen Gruppen und ggf. von der Lehrperson ergänzt. *Copy 20* kann hierzu als Musterlösung herangezogen werden.

Schritt 3:
In einem letzten Schritt verfassen die Schülerinnen und Schüler ihre eigene *film review* in Einzelarbeit. Aufgrund der Komplexität dieser Aufgabe bietet es sich an, eine Doppelstunde für die Arbeit einzuplanen. Die im vorherigen Unterrichtsschritt gemeinsam gesammelten Ergebnisse können dann für alle kopiert und verteilt oder im Hintergrund während der Arbeit an der eigenen *film review* projiziert werden. Wenn die eigene Filmkritik als Hausaufgabe verfasst werden soll, kann die OHP-Folie auch eingescannt und als E-Mail-Anhang an die Schüler versendet werden oder sie erhalten zu diesem Zweck *Copy 20*. Die Aufgabenstellung für diesen letzten Schritt lautet:

> Now it's time to write your own film review of *Slumdog Millionaire*. You can use the overview (*How to write a film review*) as a guide.

Die Schülerinnen und Schüler werden sich von der Struktur her vermutlich sowohl an die im Vorfeld analysierte Filmkritik halten, als auch an die im Unterricht selbst erstellte Übersicht bzw. die ausgeteilte Kopiervorlage (*Copy 20*). Da die Schülerinnen und Schüler innerhalb ihrer Filmkritik die eigene Meinung kundtun und die Ergebnisse somit höchst individuell ausfallen werden, unterbleibt die Darstellung einer erwarteten Schülerleistung an dieser Stelle.

How to write a review

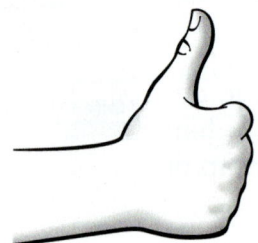

In a film review, the critic assesses a film in a reporting, i.e. factual and persuasive, style. If your job is to write a critical film review, you should include the following elements:

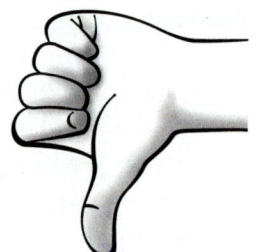

1. The most important facts of the film (the film title, the names of the director, producer, and actors, the name of the book the film is based on, etc.)
2. A short summary of the plot (approx. 3–5 sentences)
3. What you consider to be the film's strengths and weaknesses (cast, storyline, structure, music, settings, camera work, editing techniques, etc.)
4. Which characters you can identify with, which ones you reject and why
5. What the director's intention/the film's message was in your opinion
6. Whether you would recommend the film and why or why not

The structure of your review should be written in such a way as to arouse your readers' interest and it should follow this order:

- **Title**: catchy phrase
- **Opening paragraph**: comparison of this film with similar ones, focus on what's special about this film, etc.
- **Main paragraph**: plot, setting, characters; interesting details, e.g. awards, information on cast, production costs, etc.
- **Final paragraph**: conclusion, e.g. final assessment, recommendation, etc.

Make sure to provide specific examples wherever possible. Always revise your review after your first draft, checking it for spelling and language mistakes, but also to see whether you have used a clear structure and appropriate connectives and style.

Bibliographische Hinweise

Literatur:
- Ali, R. (with Anne Berthod and Divya Dugar): *Slumgirl Dreaming. My Journey to the Stars*. London: Black Swan, 2009. 101–102
- Nünning, A./Surkamp, C.: *Englische Literatur unterrichten: Grundlagen und Methoden*. Seelze-Velber: Kallmeyer/Klett, 2006. 253–256
- Swarup, V.: *Q & A*. London: Random House UK, 2006. 45–47
- Thottam, J.: "The Oscar Goes to …". *TIME* (Vol. 173, No. 10), 09/03/2009. 52.

DVDs:
- die britische DVD-Fassung des Films:
  Boyle, D.: *Slumdog Millionaire*. Pathé/Celador Films/Film4. 2008.
- die deutsche DVD-Fassung des Films:
  Boyle, D.: *Slumdog Millionaire*. Euro Video. 2009.

Internet links: *Slumdog Millionaire*
- www.impawards.com/2008/slumdog_millionaire_xlg.html
  Film poster
- www.thaindian.com/newsportal/entertainment/slumdog-title-not-offensive-but-metaphor-scriptwriter_100145447.html
  The term "Slumdog"
- www.spiegel.de/international/world/0,1518,614355,00.html
  "The Real 'Slumdog Millionaire'"
- www.thaindian.com/newsportal/uncategorized/slum-dweller-finds-slumdog-millionaire-title-abusive-sues_100145178.html
  "Slum dweller finds 'Slumdog Millionaire' title abusive, sues"
- www.asianews.it/view4print.php?l=en&art=14292
  "Enthusiasm, criticism for film 'Slumdog Millionaire'"

Internet links: Background information on India
- http://whc.unesco.org/en/list/252
- http://tourism.webindia123.com/tourism/monuments/tombs_minarets/tajmahal/index.htm
- http://asi.nic.in/asi_monu_whs_agratajmahal.asp
- www.bl.uk/learning/histcitizen/trading/bombay/history.html
- http://en.wikipedia.org/wiki/Mumbai
  Background information on Mumbai
- www.bildungsserver.hanburg.de/englisch/linkssammlungen/
- http://deutschstunden.de/Links/Englisch/Landeskunde/Indien

Bildnachweis

|action press, Hamburg: Everett Collection, Inc. 27, 27, 27, 27, 27. |Berghahn, Matthias, Bielefeld: 31, 44, 44, 88, 88. |Domke, Franz-Josef, Hannover: 30, 36. |Picture-Alliance GmbH, Frankfurt/M.: Mary Evans Picture Library 3. |ullstein bild, Berlin: SIPA 27.

Wir arbeiten sehr sorgfältig daran, für alle verwendeten Abbildungen die Rechteinhaberinnen und Rechteinhaber zu ermitteln. Sollte uns dies im Einzelfall nicht vollständig gelungen sein, werden berechtigte Ansprüche selbstverständlich im Rahmen der üblichen Vereinbarungen abgegolten.

EinFach Englisch
Unterrichtsmodelle

Herausgegeben von Hans Kröger
in Zusammenarbeit mit Carmen Mendez

Ausgewählte Titel der Reihe:

Bend it Like Beckham
Filmanalyse
86 S.   ISBN 978-3-14-041212-4

Dead Poets Society
Filmanalyse
67 S.   ISBN 978-3-14-041255-1

East is East
Filmanalyse
101 S.   ISBN 978-3-14-041228-5

L.A. Crash
Filmanalyse
92 S.   ISBN 978-3-14-041168-4
Interpretationshilfe:
107 S.   ISBN 978-3-14-041161-5

Political Speeches
Historical & Topical Issues
127 S.   ISBN 978-3-14-041236-0
Audio-CD: 70 Min.   ISBN 978-3-14-062409-1
Textausgabe: 132 S.   ISBN 978-3-14-041234-6

Slumdog Millionaire
Filmanalyse
90 S.   ISBN 978-3-14-041189-9

Utopia and Dystopia
Exploring Alternative Worlds
92 S.   ISBN 978-3-14-041204-9
Textausgabe: 92 S.   ISBN 978-3-14-041202-5

Sherman Alexie: The Absolutely True Diary of a Part-Time Indian
88 S.   ISBN 978-3-14-041187-5

T. C. Boyle: The Tortilla Curtain
152 S.   ISBN 978-3-14-041278-0

Ray Bradbury: Fahrenheit 451
72 S.   ISBN 978-3-14-041214-8

Suzanne Collins: The Hunger Games
110 S.   ISBN 978-3-14-041267-4

Lee Daniels: The Butler
Filmanalyse
130 S.   ISBN 978-3-14-041279-7

F. Scott Fitzgerald: The Great Gatsby
116 S.   ISBN 978-3-14-041191-2

Mark Haddon: The Curious Incident of the Dog in the Night-Time
99 S.   ISBN 978-3-14-041252-0

Lorraine Hansberry: A Raisin in the Sun
98 S.   ISBN 978-3-14-041241-4

Hanif Kureishi: My Son the Fanatic
80 S.   ISBN 978-3-14-041280-3

Harper Lee: To Kill a Mockingbird
108 S.   ISBN 978-3-14-041213-1

Arthur Miller: The Crucible
87 S.   ISBN 978-3-14-041270-4

Arthur Miller: Death of a Salesman
90 S.   ISBN 978-3-14-041175-2

Greg Mortenson, David Oliver Relin: Three Cups of Tea
123 S.   ISBN 978-3-14-041281-0

Jeannette Walls: Half Broke Horses
126 S.   ISBN 978-3-14-041169-1
Textausgabe:
215 S.   ISBN 978-3-14-041164-6
Interpretationshilfe:
104 S.   ISBN 978-3-14-041162-2

Die Reihe wird fortgesetzt!

Schöningh Verlag
Postfach 2540
33055 Paderborn

Schöningh westermann

Fordern Sie unseren Prospekt zur kompletten Reihe an:
Informationen 0800 / 18 18 787 (freecall)
info@westermanngruppe.de /
www.verlage.westermanngruppe.de/schoeningh